# The Case against Johann Reuchlin: *Religious and Social Controversy in Sixteenth-Century Germany*

# The Case against Johann Reuchlin

## *Religious and Social Controversy in Sixteenth-Century Germany*

Erika Rummel

UNIVERSITY OF TORONTO PRESS
Toronto Buffalo London

Toronto Buffalo London
Printed in Canada

ISBN 0-8020-3651-1 (cloth)
ISBN 0-8020-8484-2 (paper)

Printed on acid-free paper

**National Library of Canada Cataloguing in Publication Data**

Rummel, Erika, 1942–
The case against Johann Reuchlin : religious and social controversy in sixteenth-century Germany / Erika Rummel.

Includes bibliographical references and index.
ISBN 0-8020-3651-1 (bound). – ISBN 0-8020-8484-2 (pbk.)

1. Reuchlin, Johann, 1455–1522. 2. Christianity and other religions – Judaism. 3. Judaism – Relations – Christianity. 4. Jewish literature – Germany – Censorship – History – 16th century. 5. Humanism – Germany – History – 16th century. 6. Scholasticism – Germany – History – 16th century. I. Title.

B785.R64R84 2002 261.2'6'092 C2002-901295-3

The publication of this book was greatly facilitated by the generous support of the Renaissance Society of America.

University of Toronto Press acknowledges the financial assistance to its publishing program of the Canada Council for the Arts and the Ontario Arts Council.

University of Toronto Press acknowledges the financial support for its publishing activities of the Government of Canada through the Book Publishing Industry Development Program (BPIDP).

# Contents

**PREFACE**

# Cultural Bias and Historiography

The Reuchlin affair, a cause célèbre in the sixteenth century, presents an object lesson in cultural diversity. Reading about the radically different interpretations the protagonists put on the same set of events, we break through the 'crust of unity,' the cultural consensus that was once thought to define an era.[1] Until the middle of the twentieth century historians were searching for a coherent, synoptic view and therefore tended to impose on the past a grid of their own making. In neatly packaged presentations, 'The Renaissance' followed upon 'The Middle Ages,' and 'The Reformation' was contrasted with 'The Counter-Reformation.' Such broad categories, still prevalent in textbooks, are useful for organizational purposes, but imply an internal consistency and a cultural uniformity that did not exist. A study of the Reuchlin affair easily dispels such notions and opens a window on the degree of dissent present in sixteenth-century society. The tensions surface in the polemics surrounding the affair. The protagonists agreed on the facts but not on their meaning,[2] and variously portrayed the controversy as a battle between orthodox Christians and Judaizers, between Catholics and reformers, or between representatives of scholasticism and champions of humanism. The diversity of interpretations reflects the diversity of their cultural assumptions.

Part A of this book tells the story as it unfolded in 1509 when Johann Pfefferkorn, a Jewish convert, approached Emperor Maximilian I with a proposal to confiscate and destroy Jewish books. He argued that they were insulting to the Christian religion and an obstacle to the conversion of the Jews. With the approval of the emperor he set about confiscating books in Frankfurt, but the archbishop of Mainz saw these activities as an infringement on his jurisdiction and requested that due process be followed. An imperial commission, chaired by the archbishop, was established therefore to reexamine Pfefferkorn's proposals. All members of the commission, with the exception of the jurist Johann Reuchlin, strongly endorsed the initiative. In the end, however, the emperor decided against taking further action. Thus Pfefferkorn's campaign came to an end, but Reuchlin's troubles were just beginning. In his report he had cited Pfefferkorn's writings as examples of ignorant ranting and hatemongering. A polemic ensued in which the two men traded insults. Reuchlin cast doubts on Pfefferkorn's motives and deplored his lack of education; Pefferkorn in turn accused his opponent of Judaizing. In the report, Reuchlin had insisted moreover that a knowledge of Hebrew was necessary for the correct interpretation of the Bible. Attempts to do so without language skills, he said, had caused theologians to commit ridiculous errors. These remarks were offensive to Reuchlin's fellow commissioners, most of whom did not know Hebrew and did not like having their authority questioned. The conflict therefore widened. In 1513 the regional inquisitor, Jacob Hoogstraten, a member of the imperial commission and, as it happened, also of the faculty of theology at Cologne, cited Reuchlin before his court on charges of Judaizing. Reuchlin, however, appealed the citation and obtained a change of venue. The case was moved to the episcopal court of Speyer.

The initial campaign against Jewish books, the ensuing polemic, and the proceedings against Reuchlin were depicted by Pfefferkorn and his supporters as a campaign against Jews and Judaizers. In their writings, the Reuchlin affair took on the character of a crusade. Reuchlin rejected this interpretation of events and supplied an interpretation of his own, intimating that another issue was at stake: the preservation or destruction of historical sources. In Reuchlin's eyes this pitted scholars, who respected books as cultural witnesses, against boors, who had no appreciation for them, or more specifically, it pitted Reuchlin the humanist against Pfefferkorn and his supporters, the scholastic theologians of Cologne.

Confrontations between theologians and representatives of other disciplines, loosely styled 'humanists,' were endemic to German universities in Reuchlin's time. The meaning of the term 'humanist' had undergone considerable modification in Reuchlin's lifetime, changing from a professional designation to a cultural affiliation. In fifteenth-century Italy, a *humanista* was a teacher of the humanities; in sixteenth-century Germany, the term was no longer limited to any particular profession or discipline. It applied to anyone who admired and emulated the artistic and literary standards of classical antiquity. In the context of university studies, being a humanist meant promoting the study of ancient languages over Aristotelian logic, the traditional core subject, and privileging rhetorical and philological methods over scholastic dialectic. In the debate over the merits of the two systems at German universities, the protagonists soon developed a typology of the enemy. Scholastics referred to humanists as 'poets' fretting over words and endorsing semi-pagan ideas. Humanists, in turn, called the scholastics 'sophists' and characterized them as obscurantists who spoke atrocious Latin and as solipsists who had no respect for other disciplines.

Reuchlin perceived his case as the latest instance in a long series of confrontations between humanists and theologians. In fact, he saw his case as paradigmatic. As soon as the scholastic theologians were done with him, he wrote, they would 'gag all poets, one after another.'[3] Reuchlin's interpretation was readily embraced by other humanists, who rallied around him and began a letter-writing campaign to mobilize public opinion against the theologians. In 1514 Reuchlin published a selection of these letters under the title *Letters of Famous Men*. At the same time the court case was going forward at Speyer, ending in his acquittal in March 1514. The inquisitor, however, immediately appealed the verdict to the papal court in Rome, where it languished for the next six years. In 1515 another collection of letters was published, entitled *Letters of Obscure Men*. It appeared to be a scholastic response to the *Letters of Famous Men*, but on closer inspection turned out to be a satire on scholastic theology. The letters were fictitious; the authors remained anonymous.[4] They frequently referred to the anti-Judaic angle put on the Reuchlin affair, but only to ridicule the Cologne theologians and point out the irony inherent in the fact that they supported Pfefferkorn, an ethnic Jew, while manifesting a paranoid fear of all things Jewish. The authors clearly did not believe that the Reuchlin affair was a case of anti-Judaism. In their view, scholarship, not orthodoxy, was the issue. The majority of letters accordingly dealt with academic concerns: examination standards, course contents, ranking of disciplines, the enmity of the theologians toward humanists, their fear of losing students and of suffering a loss of prestige and income.

The *Letters of Obscure Men* played an important role in shifting the emphasis in the polemic from the theological to the academic sphere, from the construct that made the Reuchlin affair a case of anti-Judaism to a second construct that made it an example of the humanist-scholastic debate. The authors made a concerted effort to establish a pattern of confrontation between humanists and scholastic theologians. Many of the letters therefore contained lists of names and cases suggesting that there was a continuous history of confrontation from the fifteenth century to their own time, culminating in polemics involving contemporaries like Willibald Pirckheimer, Desiderius Erasmus, Ulrich von Hutten, and Reuchlin. Readers who perused the book when it was published no doubt identified the men listed as 'humanists.' A few years later, however, many of the men named there had, rightly or wrongly, become associated in the public mind with the Reformation. Those who read the satire in the 1520s, after Luther's rise to prominence and his condemnation by church and state, could easily conclude therefore that humanists and reformers shared a common platform and that Reuchlin and Luther were victims of the same party. Thus the *Letters of Obscure Men* served not only as a means of shifting the interpretation of the Reuchlin affair from the idea that it was a case of anti-Judaism to the idea that it was a confrontation between humanists and scholastics, but also pointed readers in the direction of a third construct: that the Reuchlin affair had much in common with the Luther affair. Luther's own writings prepared the way for this retro-interpretation of Reuchlin's case as a pre-Reformation controversy. He explicitly linked his own case to Reuchlin's. The Cologne theologians, he said, were smarting from the defeat they had suffered in their battle against Reuchlin. To save face and regain their old standing, they started agitating against Luther. Shortly afterwards, in May 1520, the papal court rendered the final verdict in the Reuchlin case: the acquittal was overturned, and Reuchlin was obliged to pay the court costs. His scholarly reputation remained unimpaired, however. He accepted a position at the University of Tübingen, where he taught Greek and Hebrew until his death two years later, in 1522.

In the following chapters (1–3), the three interpretations of the Reuchlin affair current in the sixteenth century will be examined in more detail. Chapter 1 will give an account of Pfefferkorn's life and works and discuss the anti-Judaic facets of the case. Chapter 2 will focus on the arguments of Reuchlin and his supporters and discuss the case under the heading of the humanist-scholastic debate. Chapter 3 will examine the events that led to a reinterpretation of the Reuchlin affair as a pre-Reformation controversy. The question whether these sixteenth-century interpretations reflected spontaneous judgments and genuine convictions or were purposely constructed and used for strategic purposes is the subject of chapter 4. The concluding chapter 5 will examine the place of the Reuchlin affair in modern historiography.

In the 1970s Golo Mann observed: 'Historiography has become modest; it no longer searches for the great meaning.'[5] He attributed the reduced scope of historical inquiry to epistemological doubts and the realization that the quest for a value-free account of past events was a pipe dream. As it became accepted wisdom that every age imposes its own cultural assumptions on the sources, historians fell back on documentary realism and microhistory, approaching the study of culture 'through single, seemingly insignificant, signs, rather than through the application of laws derived from repeatable and quantifiable observations.'[6] Microhistory of course presents its own difficulties. The topical, and therefore apparently more manageable, choice of a microcosm over a complex universe does not allow us to achieve closure or approach new levels of accuracy that were elusive on a larger scale. The problem of writing about discourse without participating in it remains unresolved, but this book seeks to provide an antidote to the subjectivity inherent in any mediating narrative by supplying the texts on which the narrative is based.[7] At the very least, this allows readers to evaluate the account given here and to balance the author's aesthetic and moral ground with their own.[8]

Part B supplies extracts from source texts that shed light on the affair: two pamphlets by Pfefferkorn, one full of virulent, anti-semitic rhetoric (*The Enemy of the Jews*), the other containing surprisingly authentic descriptions of Jewish rites (*The Confession of the Jews*); two tracts by Reuchlin, one containing his report to the imperial commission, the other his *Defence Against the Cologne Slanderers*; a selection from the *Letters of Obscure Men*; and an assortment of epistolary exchanges and official judgments that illustrate the opinions of faculties of theology at German universities and of well-known humanists and reformers such as Erasmus, Pirckheimer, Hutten, and Luther. Many of the texts are not available in critical modern editions and have been translated into English here for the first time. Headnotes to individual sources will provide the necessary background information.

## Notes

1 C. Ginzburg, *The Cheese and the Worms* (Baltimore, 1980), 20, uses the expression 'breaking the crust of religious unity.'

2 The most recent study is Hans Peterse, *Jacobus Hoogstraeten gegen Johannes Reuchlin: Ein Beitrag zur Geschichte des Antijudaismus im 16. Jahrhundert* (Mainz, 1995). English readers will find a good account and discussion of the Reuchlin affair in James Overfield, *Humanism and Scholasticism in Late Medieval Germany* (Princeton, 1984), 247–97. The classic account is L. Geiger's biography of Reuchlin, *Reuchlin: Sein Leben und seine Werke* (Leipzig, 1871; repr. Nieuwkoop 1964). These and other accounts of the Reuchlin affair are discussed in more detail below, 36–40.

3 G. Friedlaender, ed., *Beiträge zur Reformationsgeschichte: Sammlung ungedruckter Briefe des Reuchlin, Beza und Bullinger* (Berlin, 1837), 47

4 *Epistolae obscurorum virorum* (1515); see excerpts below, 109–27. The principal authors of this collaborative work were Crotus Rubeanus and Ulrich von Hutten.

5 *Propyläen Weltgeschichte: Eine Universalgeschichte* (Frankfurt, 1976), XI–2: 522.

6 E. Muir, 'Introduction: Observing Trifles,' in E. Muir and G. Ruggiero, eds., *Microhistory and the Lost Peoples of Europe* (Baltimore, 1991), xxi.

7 Cf. G. Levi, 'On Microhistory,' in P. Burke, ed., *New Perspectives on Historical Writing* (University Park, 1991), 106.

8 Hayden White declared that historical interpretations rest on 'aesthetic or moral rather than epistemological ground' in *Metahistory: The Historical Imagination in Nineteenth-Century Europe* (London, 1973), 427.

# ACKNOWLEDGMENTS

This book has been prepared with the support of the J.P. Getty Research Institute, where I was a resident scholar in 1999/2000. I owe special thanks to Ayana Haviv, who spent much time and effort transcribing the Hebrew phrases in Pfefferkorn's tracts and tracing their sources. Her help was indispensable. I would also like to thank Otniel Drohr, my first Hebrew teacher; Margaret Olin, who gave me the benefit of her encyclopedic learning; Charles Salas, who always had a friendly word for me; and Natalie Davis, who has given me encouragement throughout. Finally I would like to thank my assistant, Chris Hudson, for proofreading and correcting the manuscript, the readers of the Press, and the copy-editor, Miriam Skey, for their valuable advice. They have all contributed to 'the furniture of good learning,' *suppellex bonarum literarum*, as Reuchlin's contemporary, Erasmus, put it.

CHRONOLOGY

# The Reuchlin Affair

1504 Johann Pfefferkorn converts to Christianity.

1509 Pfefferkorn advocates the destruction of Jewish books to facilitate the conversion of Jews to Christianity.

1510 Emperor Maximilian appoints a commission to examine Pfefferkorn's proposals.

1511 The commission, consisting mostly of theology professors, recommends in favour of destroying Hebrew books. Johann Reuchlin, a legal expert and a scholar of Hebrew, gives the only dissenting opinion. The emperor does not act on the recommendation of the commission. Reuchlin and Pfefferkorn engage in a polemic. Pfefferkorn publishes the *Hand Mirror*; Reuchlin replies with the *Eye Mirror*.

1513 The theologians at the University of Cologne support Pfefferkorn and condemn the *Eye Mirror*. Reuchlin is cited before a court of the Inquisition on charges of Judaism. He publishes a *Defence against the Cologne Slanderers* and challenges the citation on legal grounds. The case is moved to the episcopal court of Speyer.

1514 Humanists take up Reuchlin's defense in a letter campaign (published as *Letters of Famous Men*). The court of appeal decides in Reuchlin's favour. The inquisitor launches a counterappeal to the papal court in Rome.

1515 A second, anonymous collection of letters, *Letters of Obscure Men*, appears. The letters purport to defend the position of the theologians, but turn out to be fictitious. The book is a humanistic satire on scholastic theologians.

1517 Luther publishes the Ninety-five Theses; a second, enlarged edition of *Letters of Obscure Men* appears.

1518 Luther publishes the *Resolutions of the Disputations Concerning the Efficacy of Indulgences*, linking his case with Reuchlin's.

1520 The papal court condemns and fines Reuchlin. Luther, now threatened with excommunication, publishes the *Response to the Doctrinal Condemnation by the Louvain and Cologne Theologians*, again linking his case with Reuchlin.

1522 Reuchlin enters the priesthood shortly before his death in June.

# Part A

# THE REUCHLIN AFFAIR IN CONTEXT

CHAPTER 1

# Pfefferkorn and the Battle against Judaism[1]

Josef Pfefferkorn, who changed his name to 'Johann' when he converted to Christianity in 1504, was a Moravian Jew. He lived for a while in Prague, then moved to Nürnberg, and finally settled in Cologne. Information about his life is sketchy and comes primarily from incidental remarks in his own writings and those of Reuchlin. The polemical context of these remarks makes them suspect, but external evidence is scant and equally problematic. There are a number of official documents, safe-conducts and testimonials, but they contradict each other, some attesting to Pfefferkorn's good character, others accusing him of criminal activity. In 1514 a broadsheet was circulating that identified him with a Jew by the name of Pfefferkorn who had been convicted of theft and executed.[2] Pfefferkorn, who was alive and well, complained that 'two Jews wanted to sully my reputation with a charge of theft ... I cited them before the imperial court, and they were obliged to pay thirty gold florins to cover my expenses and had to retract the accusations in public.'[3] The episode illustrates the unreliability of the extant sources.

It is not clear what Pfefferkorn did for a living before his conversion. One document suggests that he was a butcher; he himself denies it without specifying his profession.[4] Modern historians speculate that he was a moneylender. After his conversion Pfefferkorn earned his living as a missionary among Jews, travelling in the central and southern regions of the Empire between 1504, when he is documented at Dachau, and 1509, when he settled in Cologne. His success appears to have been modest, however. In 1516 he declared that he had converted fourteen Jews, claiming that five more would have been baptized if Reuchlin had not blackened his name.[5] Pfefferkorn's Dominican mentors also permitted him to address Christian congregations in Cologne. Reuchlin protested against this practice, pointing out that preaching was a privilege reserved for members of the clergy, but Pfefferkorn countered that he had never spoken about matters of faith. He had confined himself to topics that could be legitimately discussed by laymen. He had argued against usury and urged that Jews be forced to listen to Christian sermons.[6] In 1513 Pfefferkorn obtained a permanent position as hospital warden of St Ursula's in Cologne. He is last documented there in 1521.[7]

Pfefferkorn was married and had a son. Both his wife, Anna, and his son, Laurentius, converted to Christianity. Laurentius, who 'studiously devoted himself to the liberal disciplines and the poets,' occasionally assisted his father with his editorial tasks.[8] The question of Pfefferkorn's own education was repeatedly raised by Reuchlin. He depicted Pfefferkorn as an ignoramus and alleged that his pamphlets had been produced with substantial input from the theologians of Cologne.[9] Pfefferkorn denied that they had been involved in any significant way. He claimed that his own resources were sufficient for the purpose. He had received his early education from his uncle, Rabbi Meir Pfefferkorn. It was true that he knew only German and Hebrew. People might therefore ask: 'How can Pfefferkorn cite Holy Writ and canon law and the sayings of Latin writers when he does not know Latin? I reply that this objection is futile ... I carry with me a pen and writing tablet and I am able to note down what I hear in public sermons or in the assemblies of learned men. How many sermons delivered by doctors and men in holy orders have I heard over the last twelve years! How many admonitions! How many authoritative quotations from the holy Fathers, which I could either retain in my memory or ask about and note down! I am reasonably confident, moreover, (for I do not want to brag) that I can cite anything that is either in the Bible or in the holy gospels on my own strength, without the help of an interpreter, and can give authorities for any subject, in German or Hebrew. And I want to add: I have learned by heart all the gospels that are throughout the year explained to the congregation in the church of God and I have learned to recite them accurately.'[10] Pfefferkorn, then, prided himself on his excellent memory. As Reuchlin pointed out, however, his translations of the Hebrew prooftexts cited in his pamphlets were flawed, which allowed only two interpretations: either Pfefferkorn's knowledge was inadequate or he was deliberately misleading his readers. It remains unclear, moreover, to what extent

Pfefferkorn, who wrote his pamphlets in German, had control over the Latin versions, which appeared in quick succession and often differed significantly from the original. He suppressed the identity of the translator in all but one case,[11] obviously wishing to give the impression that he was responsible for the final form. In the *Beschyrmung* (Defence) a tract published in 1516, he comments explicitly on this point: 'I had the German book translated into Latin with several additions here and there, according to my own wishes and pleasure. I listened as it was repeatedly recited to me word for word. And I had it printed thus. And I am prepared to speak and answer for it myself to anyone and before the whole world. I attested to this before a notary and witnesses.'[12] In answer to Reuchlin's charge that he was an ignoramus he gleefully referred to the scholar's troubles with the inquisitorial court: 'Which of us is the better man is known only to God who has no regard for high-sounding speech and rhetorical flourishes and looks only at the naked truth. This much I can say about myself without bragging: My books have not been condemned by any university.'[13]

In many ways Pfefferkorn's life exemplifies a convert's difficulties in integrating into the Christian community. A certain reluctance prevailed among Christians to accept the changed status of a convert. Viktor von Karben, a fellow convert, reported that Christians 'mocked, derided, and pointed fingers at them, and said of individual men: "Look, here comes the baptized Jew." There are Christians, moreover, who accost them with insults, saying that there was no use in helping them because they had never met a Jew who was any good.'[14] Jews who adhered to their faith incurred both systemic discrimination and personal danger from a population that was xenophobic and had a lynch mentality. In secular law, Jews were designated 'servants' of the empire, and subject to the imperial law. This was based on the theological concept that the Jewish synagogue had been subjugated by the Christian church. Church laws envisaged complete segregation between Jews and Christians, and legislation to this effect was passed by the Council of Basel (1431–49). This proved unenforceable in practice, but social intercourse between Jews and Christians was tightly regulated. Jews were required to wear special clothing or identifying badges and to keep a curfew on certain Christian feast days. Town guilds refused to accept Jews as members, which limited their sphere of activity to the field of finance, wholesale commerce, and the practice of medicine. Even in those areas, their activities were controlled by laws favouring the Christian community. They were subject to surtaxes and, on conversion, had to relinquish a part of their assets to atone for their acquisition through usury.[15] The predominance of Jews in the business of moneylending exposed them to resentment, and religion often became a pretext for venting it. Sermons against usury, which was forbidden to Christians, lent themselves to anti-Jewish rhetoric, converting theological arguments into arguments against Jewish business practices. Superstition, in the form of beliefs that Jews kidnapped and killed Christian children and desecrated the host, and other scurrilous accusations added to the precarious position of Jews living in a society dominated by Christian values.[16]

During the fifteenth century European Jews suffered a series of pogroms. The political fragmentation of the German empire meant, however, that they were not subjected to wholesale expulsion as they were in states with a centralized government, such as England and Spain. The Jews were, however, expelled from individual German cities and territories and forced to take up residence in the surrounding countryside or in neighbouring jurisdictions. Their expulsion served the political interests of cities and territorial rulers because it eliminated opportunities for interference by the emperor, whose nominal subjects the Jews were. During the same time the economic importance of the Jews, which had given them a measure of protection, was gradually reduced as Christian bankers were permitted to charge interest under the guise of administrative charges or reimbursement for lost income.

In the sixteenth century, as humanism began to shape the intellectual climate in Germany, the status quo in culture, politics, and society became the subject of intensive scrutiny and criticism. Although the humanists' challenge to medieval authorities is often portrayed as a plea for tolerance, it is more accurate to say that the old order was replaced with an equally restrictive new order. The humanists were by no means champions of Jewish emancipation. The Dutch humanist Desiderius Erasmus displayed a certain sympathy, declaring ironically: 'If it is Christian to detest the Jews, we are all good Christians, and to spare.'[17] This did not keep him, however, from supporting anti-Semitic clichés in his comments on the Reuchlin affair. Thus he said of Pfefferkorn: 'Now that he has put on the mask of the Christian, he truly plays the Jew. Now at last he is true to his race. They have slandered Christ, but Christ only. He raves against many upright men of proven virtue and learning.'[18] The same tensions characterize Reuchlin's attitude toward the Jews. On the one hand he expressed the greatest respect for his Hebrew teacher, Iacob ben Iehiel Loans, whom he addressed in a letter as his 'lord and master, guide and friend,' words that prompted Pfefferkorn to exclaim: 'If I had written this, I would probably be burned!'[19] On the other hand, a tract entitled *Why the Jews Have Lived in Misery for So Long* (1505), repeats the conventional view that they were justly suffering for the sins of their forefathers who had murdered Jesus, and were paying for their own stubborn refusal to convert to Christianity.[20] Most humanists, like Erasmus and Reuchlin, shared in the prejudices of their time. Their attitude was modified only by an appreciation for source texts in Hebrew, Greek, and Latin, and resulted in their promotion of language studies, including Hebrew. If they served Jewish interests, it was on the basis of cultural politics rather than the principle of toleration. Nor did Jews find acceptance or support among the reformers, whose movement was as important and perhaps more consequential than humanism.

Luther's tract *Jesus Christ Was Born a Jew* (1523) was not simply a defence of Jewish liberties, but rather an attack on the tyranny of the Catholic church and it was driven by the expectation that the Jews would find common ground with the reformers and convert to their brand of Christianity. He reasoned somewhat naively that Jews clung to their faith because they had been maltreated by Christians. Those 'fools, the papists, bishops, sophists, and monks have hitherto so dealt with the Jews that every good Christian would have preferred to be a Jew. If I had been a Jew and received such treatment ... I'd rather have been a pig than a Christian.' In Luther's view, all that was needed was a change in attitude. If the Jews were treated kindly, they would embrace Christianity.[21] When this did not come to pass, Luther reversed his position and wrote a series of anti-Semitic tracts, beginning in 1538 with *Against the Sabbatarians*, in which he accused the Jews of propagating heresies, and culminating in the pamphlet *Of the Jews and Their Lies* (1543), in which he called for the destruction of their synagogues and the confiscation of their books, stopping short only of advocating murder. The Catholic emperor, Charles V, by contrast was careful not to alienate the Jews in the ensuing wars of religion and benefited from his diplomatic stance. His benevolence was to a large extent politically motivated. As king of Spain (and before his election to the imperial throne which made him the legal overlord of the Jews), the fifteen-year-old had urged the pope to condemn Reuchlin as a Judaizer. After his election in 1519, he assumed a cautiously neutral position. In 1530 he invited Jewish scholars to debate with the convert Antonius Margarita, who had revived the hostile notions of Pfefferkorn and claimed that Jewish writings were subversive. Accepting the defence of Jewish scholars, Charles turned against Margarita and had him arrested as a disturber of the peace. In 1547, during the war against the Protestant League of Schmalkalden, Jewish communities contributed financially to the emperor's campaign and prayed for his victory. He renewed their privileges and promised them protection in the wake of the religious settlement (Peace of Augsburg, 1555), which guaranteed princes the right to determine confessional matters in their realm.[22]

Efforts to convert Jews to Christianity were spearheaded in Germany as elsewhere by the Dominican and Franciscan orders, but converts themselves often played an important role in the process. In the second half of the fifteenth century and at the beginning of the sixteenth century, a spate of missionary tracts appeared in Germany. Among the most prominent was the Dominican Petrus Nigri's *Star of Messiah* (Latin 1475, German 1477) and the works of two converts: Viktor von Karben's *On the Life and Manners of Jews* (1509), and Antonius Margarita's *The Whole Jewish Faith* (1531). Pfefferkorn's own publications belong to the same tradition. His tone varies from accusatory and malignant to factual and even solicitous. One of his first publications entitled, *The Enemy of the Jews,* was stridently anti-Semitic.[23] In the first section of the book Pfefferkorn claimed that Jews used insulting and blasphemous epithets in references to Jesus, Mary, and the apostles; and that they hated Christians, cursed and execrated them, and daily prayed for their destruction. To prove his point, he quoted epithets and prayers in Hebrew, adding a transliteration as well as a translation. He spoke with the air of a man giving away secrets, telling of things 'concealed for a long time and now published and brought to light in their own Hebrew language and script, translated into German.'[24] Pfefferkorn's style is unsophisticated but rhetorically effective. In the second section, entitled 'How the Jews ruin land and people,' he makes clever use of dialogue, presenting a conversation between a pawnbroker and his client that depicts the Jew as scheming and greedy, the Christian as the wretched victim of dubious business practices. To demonstrate the effects of usury, he gives a year-by-year account of the debt accumulating on 1 Gulden lent at '6 Cologne Weisspfennig and 1 Heller a week.' After thirty years the debt amounts to an unfathomable 106 tons of gold, 14,810 Gulden, 28 Weisspfennig and 11 Heller! 'Thus the poor Christian, when he has nothing further to pawn, must run away and live out his life in poverty, which happens often and many times.'[25] He concluded the book with an appeal to the authorities to regulate the lives of the Jews more tightly. He urged them to put an end to usurious practices, to deprive the Jews of their ill-gotten gains, to force them into lowly occupations, and confiscate all their books with the exception of the Bible. Deprived of their books, Jews would adopt a different attitude, he said. They would abandon their 'false' beliefs and embrace Christianity.

Occasionally Pfefferkorn manifests conflicting emotions, appealing to his Christian readers to make the Jews their brothers in the faith, and at the same time inciting hatred against them. Combining his contradictory desires in one and the same sentence, he expresses the hope that 'the corrupt race will be zealously resisted and disdained and ... enlightened and led to the right understanding.'[26] Other double-edged remarks in his writings similarly reveal a man torn between old and new loyalties. In his first publication in 1507, *Speculum adhortationis Iudaice ad Christum* (Mirror of Exhortation to Turn Jews to Christ), the conflicting desires – to save but also to punish the Jews– are particularly evident. Pfefferkorn first addresses himself to the Jews directly, exhorting them to convert to Christianity, and then turns to Christian authorities, urging them to motivate Jews to abandon their native religion by imposing punitive measures. He notes that the authorities have imposed a surtax on Jews for just this purpose. He now suggests another, in his view more effective, measure: depriving them of the books that instruct them in their 'heresy.' Why not do the Jews a good turn, he asks, even if it will not yield a financial profit as surtaxes do?[27] This ironic twist reveals a faultline in the author's reasoning that is indicative of inner tension. The moment of irony interrupts the speech pattern, breaks into the missionary rhetoric, and reveals Pfefferkorn's feelings of alienation from Christian society. Two tracts describing Jewish rites offer an even clearer indication of the conflict between his desire to convert his former coreligionists and the nostalgia he may have felt for a tradition familiar to him from childhood on. The two tracts, entitled *Jewish Confession* (Cologne 1508) and *How the Blind Jews Keep Easter* (Cologne 1509), represent a new type of literature about Jewish customs and rites, which belongs to the genre of social history. Although critical of Jewish beliefs and written as a tool for conversion, these tracts, which describe Rosh Hashanah, Yom Kippur, and Passover ceremonies, offer straightforward descriptions that transcend propaganda purposes and have a certain authenticity. This is evident not only from the text but also from several illustrations remarkable for their departure from traditional iconography in which Jews are generally depicted as murderers of Christ and enemies of Christianity.

In the text itself, anti-Jewish rhetoric stands side by side with descriptive passages that are free of ideology and even convey a certain sympathy for the Jews. Thus references to the 'vain fantasies' of the Jews are tempered with the acknowledgment that they showed great piety and devotion in the performance of rites. And, whereas Pfefferkorn elsewhere describes Jews in a stereotypical way as devious and fraudulent, they appear in these two tracts as sincere believers: 'They are completely convinced and do not doubt that their hands are endowed with the spirit of the Lord.'[28] Such positive evaluations are incidental, however, to his declared purpose which is to disparage and reproach the Jews. 'This is my purpose,' he declares: 'that they may be mocked and reproved for this custom and perhaps abandon their errors on account of the ridicule and be moved to turn to the light of the Christian faith.'[29]

Pfefferkorn saw the confiscation and destruction of Jewish books, especially the Talmud, as an important preliminary step to converting the Jews and in almost every one of his publications urged the authorities to take appropriate measures. In an interview with the archbishop of Mainz he insisted that 'their false books, which their rabbis have written against the holy gospel and to disgrace, insult, defame, and blaspheme our holy faith, played a key role in making them obstinate.'[30] In 1509 he took more concrete steps, making formal application to the imperial court to have them confiscated. Kunikunde von Bayern, the devout sister of Emperor Maximilian I, promoted his efforts. She provided a letter of introduction to the emperor, who endorsed Pfefferkorn's proposals and authorized him to confiscate any Jewish books that insulted the Christian religion and violated Old Testament law.[31] It was unusual for an individual who had no official rank to receive such a mandate, and the emperor's action drew immediate protests both from Jewish representatives and from Uriel of Gemmingen, the archbishop of Mainz. In deference to the archbishop, who suggested that 'Johannes Pfefferkorn was neither learned nor experienced enough' for the task, Maximilian decided to revisit the matter. He expressly stated that the mandate he had given Pfefferkorn remained in force, but 'to avoid any complaints on the part of the Jews that this had been undertaken lightly and without diligent consideration' he authorized the archbishop to solicit reports on the matter from four universities (Mainz, Cologne, Erfurt, Heidelberg) as well as from qualified individuals.[32]

By the end of the year, the reports were in. The commissioners recommended in favour of Pfefferkorn's proposal; Reuchlin wrote the only dissenting opinion. Pfefferkorn reported triumphantly: 'All, with the exception of Johann Reuchlin, unanimously declared and wrote for Christ, inspired by the Holy Spirit. His report alone ... supported the perfidy of the Jews rather than the apostolic See and the most holy cause of our faith.' When Reuchlin wrote that report, he said, using a picturesque metaphor, 'a fat Jew sat on his book.' He repeatedly called Reuchlin a 'Judas' and a 'half-Jew.' He would not have believed 'that there was such perfidy among Christians.'[33] The four universities recommended that all Jewish books be confiscated and examined by qualified theologians. Those considered dangerous or blasphemous were to be burned; the rest were to be returned to their owners. A certain number of copies of the condemned books would be deposited in designated libraries and reserved for the use of scholars. The universities also recommended that the practice of usury be stopped and Jews be permitted and encouraged to practise trades now reserved for Christians. They should be kept from practising usury and admitted to take up 'honest work,' but they should be distinguished from Christians by wearing a clearly visible badge.[34] The examination of the Jewish books involved a complicated bureaucratic process. The title of every confiscated book had to be listed in two registers by a notary public, one to be left with Jewish authorities, the other to be deposited in the imperial archive. Clearly it was not an easy task to separate supposedly harmful from innocuous books and, to forestall complaints, scholars versed in Hebrew and with impeccable Christian credentials would have to be found who could pass judgment on the books.[35]

The archbishop forwarded the suggestions of the commission to the emperor, personally supporting the recommendation of the theologians, but Maximilian chose not to act on it. He may have decided that the ends did not justify the means, or he may have been swayed by Jewish leaders lobbying his court. They negotiated with him throughout the winter of 1509 and in the spring of 1510 they finally achieved their goal. The confiscated books were returned. Pfefferkorn fulminated that 'the Jews bribed Christians in high places ... and they filled the ears of the good Emperor with false advice, so that His Imperial Majesty gave orders to restore the books to the Jews.' The need for bribery is confirmed by letters from the delegate of the Frankfurt Jews, Jonathan Levi Zion, who visited the imperial court near Padua. In the days leading up to his audience, he was trying to raise funds and urging his community to supply him with money. He 'feared to come before the Emperor empty-handed, for ... it is almost certain that I shall achieve nothing.' 'Only God and our own wallets can save us,' he said. When the emperor appointed the margrave of Baden to look into the matter, Zion reported that he 'gave him something' on the spot and promised more: 'If he should obtain what we are asking for in our petition, I shall give him an additional one hundred Gulden for his efforts.'[36] Pfefferkorn was bitterly disappointed by the emperor's failure to proceed with his plan. In his opinion the decision would have grave consequences: 'The Jews were not only confirmed in their opposition to us Christians, but even said to me: "Reuchlin knows how to deal with you and oppose you." ... They told me that they were in close contact with Reuchlin and very well informed about this matter. Then I ... remembered the German proverb: "Learning corrupts."'[37] The Jews, he said, were overjoyed. He had heard that they held a celebration and fashioned two images, 'one of Johann Reuchlin in angelic form, like a prophet; the other, of Pfefferkorn, in the shape of a devil.' They danced around the images like pagans around a sacrifice, genuflecting to Reuchlin's image and sticking knives into Pfefferkorn's.[38] Pfefferkorn's indignation was shared by the Inquisitor Jacob Hoogstraten. He refrained from accusing the Jewish delegation of bribing the court but noted the implications of their successful lobbying: 'If the Jews are permitted to retain the books that have been taken from them by imperial mandate, they will be confirmed in their perfidy, they will insult Christians, and cast it in their teeth that the books would not have been restored to them by imperial edict if they were not true and holy.'[39]

Pfefferkorn first made contact with Reuchlin in 1510, when he visited the scholar for a private consultation. 'He treated me most cordially,' he reported, 'and expressed pleasure at my coming, and what is more, he instructed me in what to do in the presence of the Emperor, of which I have proof in his own handwriting. Then, when he had cleverly found out everything about the matter from me, he falsely reassured me and devoutly promised to write to me. He did no such thing, but instead traduced me in his report to His Royal Majesty, contrary to his promise and acting most impiously ... And so he betrayed me, as Judas betrayed Christ.'[40] Although Pfefferkorn had to give up his campaign to confiscate Jewish books, he continued to argue his case in a series of polemical tracts against Reuchlin. The principal arguments appear in the *Handt Spiegel* (Hand Mirror, 1511), in which Pefferkorn condemned the Talmud and inveighed against Reuchlin for having prevented its destruction, citing his report to the emperor. Reuchlin replied with the *Augenspiegel* (Eye Mirror, 1511) in which he published an annotated version of his report, accusing Pfefferkorn of having made unauthorized use of this confidential document. Reuchlin's book was condemned by the theologians of Cologne for favouring the Jews and this led to his citation before the inquisitorial court. His battle against the theologians will concern us further in the next section. Pfefferkorn carried on the vendetta, publishing a collection of texts relevant to the controversy under the title *Beschyrmung* (in Latin, *Defensio*, or Defence, 1516). It contained, among other documents, the reports of several universities recommending the confiscation of Jewish books and their verdicts on Reuchlin's *Eye Mirror*, correspondence between Reuchlin and the Cologne theologians, and Pfefferkorn's own copious notes and summaries of the events. Pfefferkorn treated the affair as a battle on behalf of orthodoxy against Judaism. Reuchlin saw it as a defence of learning against boors. Reacting to this construct in his *Defence*, Pfefferkorn fires a parting shot at his opponent: 'If someone objects, saying to me, "if you are ignorant, why do you set yourself up against a doctor of law and a humanist?" I reply ... learning is no defence against the charge of depravity. All the heretics are proof of this, for they were always the most learned men.'[41]

## CHAPTER 2

# Reuchlin and the Scholastic Theologians

So far we have followed Pfefferkorn's polemic against Reuchlin, which was partly motivated by personal rancour against a man who had portrayed him as insincere and ignorant, but also fought over the issue of orthodoxy. The controversy did not remain a personal feud for long. It soon attracted widespread public attention. The theologians of Cologne and their colleagues, especially at the universities of Mainz, Louvain, and Paris, supported Pfefferkorn's original quest and condemned Reuchlin's *Eye Mirror*. Humanists, however, came to Reuchlin's defence. While orthodoxy remained the issue in court, the involvement of humanists on Reuchlin's behalf changed the character of the public debate, shifting it to the realm of education and cultural preferences.

Johann Reuchlin was a widely respected scholar. He had studied in Freiburg, Paris, and Basel, graduating BA (1474) and MA (1477). While in Basel, he became a member of the humanistic circle at the Amerbach Press, produced a number of study aids, and composed two comedies for school use. He then returned to France, where he was tutored in Greek by the émigré Georgius Hermonymus and studied law at Orléans and Poitiers. In 1481 he matriculated at the University of Tübingen, where he continued his legal studies while teaching Greek. He obtained his doctorate in imperial law in 1484–5. By this time he had entered the service of Count Eberhard of Würtemberg as a court judge. The count also employed him on diplomatic missions that took him to Italy and to the imperial court. In recognition of his merits, the emperor raised him to the rank of hereditary nobility. When Count Eberhard died in 1496 and was succeeded by his nephew Eberhard the Younger, Reuchlin, who had been involved in efforts to curb the young count's power, found himself persona non grata. For the next two years he lived in political exile in Heidelberg, where he enjoyed the patronage of Johann von Dalburg, bishop of Worms and councillor of Philip, Elector Palatine. The following year Reuchlin travelled to Italy in the diplomatic service of Philip. In 1498 Count Eberhard was unseated in favour of Ulrich of Würtemberg, and Reuchlin returned to his home in Stuttgart. Subsequently he sat on the supreme court of Speyer and acted as legal counsel to the Swabian League, a recently founded alliance of princes, knights, and cities in southern Germany. He held this position until the headquarters of the alliance were moved to Augsburg in 1512. At that time Reuchlin, now fifty-seven years old, withdrew from public life to concentrate on humanistic studies.

Reuchlin's interest in Hebrew studies may have been awakened by contacts with Wessel Gansfort, one of the first Hebraists north of the Alps. He was confirmed in his appreciation of Hebrew scholarship and introduced to the cabala by Pico della Mirandola, whom he met on his first diplomatic mission to Italy in 1490. During the same journey he also studied Hebrew with Obadja Sforno, a physician and philosopher, and collected Hebrew manuscripts and books, still a rarity north of the Alps. On a mission to the imperial court in 1492, he met and received instruction in Hebrew from the learned court physician Iacob ben Iehiel Loans. The two men remained in contact, and over the next decade Reuchlin repeatedly expressed his admiration for Loans.[1]

In Reuchlin's time it took considerable personal initiative to acquire a knowledge of Hebrew. Neither books nor teachers were readily available. The first Hebrew Bible was printed in Soncino in 1488, but it took some years before it became available north of the Alps. There were no Jewish communities in Würtemberg, where Reuchlin might have found a teacher.[2] University lectureships were established only in the 1520s. Thus Reuchlin was largely an autodidact. He shared his knowledge informally with students in Heidelberg, stimulating interest in Hebrew studies in humanistic circles there. The first fruit of his studies was a dialogue, *De verbo mirifico* (The Wonder-Working Word, 1484), in which he tried to combine cabalistic with Christian mysticism. He also compiled a Hebrew grammar, *De rudimentis Hebraicis* (On the Rudiments of Hebrew, 1506). The grammar, which became the standard work in the field, was the first book in Germany to contain Hebrew print. The cabala remained the focus of his Hebrew studies and is the subject of the book *De arte cabalistica* (On the Cabalistic Art, 1517).

The cabala, literally 'tradition,' was a philosophical or theosophical inquiry into the nature of the divine. It was taught hermetically, that is, reserved for the elect, and was often associated with magic, a connection deplored even by Jewish teachers of stature such as Moses Maimonides. Christians began to take an interest in the cabala during the fifteenth century. The Italian humanist Pico della Mirandola was the first to attempt a fusion of the cabala with Christian teaching and to seek confirmation for Christian doctrine in the Jewish tradition. He connected the cabala with 'natural magic,' that is, the study of celestial bodies, but rejected its counterpart, black magic, 'which is rightly excised by the church and has no foundation, no truth, and no basis.'[3] His pronouncements on the merit of the cabala were, however, singled out as heterodox in inquisitorial hearings. Pico defended himself in an apologia which persuaded Pope Alexander VI to acquit him of the charges in 1493. Indeed, the study of the cabala was accepted at the papal and imperial courts as can be seen from the translations commissioned by Alexander's predecessor, Pope Sixtus IV, and the dedication of another translation by Paulus Riccius to Emperor Maximilian (*Porta lucis*, Gate of Light, 1516). Nevertheless it remained a controversial subject. It continued to attract the attention of inquisitorial courts and was therefore pursued by Reuchlin at some personal risk.

At the time of his controversy with Pfefferkorn, Reuchlin had retired to private practice and was living the life of an independent scholar in Stuttgart. Consulted on the merits of Pfefferkorn's proposal, he delivered a report that was written in an offhand manner and surprisingly candid. In retrospect, he acknowledged that his nonchalance had been unfortunate. He had failed to give any thought to the views of other commissioners and the possibility that he might be left isolated. He gave his opinion spontaneously, he said, and 'in a rhetorical manner conducive to persuasion.'[4] In other words, he had written in the style of a humanist rather than a lawyer. In the report he disparaged Pfefferkorn's proposal. He noted that, legally speaking, there was no actionable case. The Jews were subject to imperial law and entitled to the protection of the law which guaranteed the quiet enjoyment of one's private possessions. Under the provisions of imperial law, books could be legally confiscated only after a judgment had been rendered declaring that they contained libel or dealt with black magic. Since no such judgment existed against Jewish books, their confiscation was illegal. In an unusually liberal statement, Reuchlin noted that doctrinal differences did not automatically involve blasphemy. The Jews were simply professing their faith, he said, which did not constitute an insult to any other faith.[5] Reuchlin indicated, moreover, that he thought Pfefferkorn's proposal smacked of anti-Semitism. His pamphlet, *The Enemy of the Jews*, contained unsubstantiated charges and tendentious translations of Hebrew texts. 'In this manner,' Reuchlin warned, 'one may easily incite hatred against the Jews among unlearned people who do not know the language, so that their [the Jews'] lives and possessions are endangered.'[6] Pfefferkorn had stressed that ecclesiastical laws prohibited intercourse between Jews and Christians, but Reuchlin gave them a more generous interpretation. To begin with, it was clear that not all intercourse was forbidden. Christians were allowed to enter into legal and commercial relations with Jews and to learn from them matters that did not touch on the faith. More importantly, however, relations between Jews and Christians were governed by Christ's commandment to love one's neighbour.[7] In the remainder of his report Reuchlin moved beyond legal issues to concerns that were closer to his heart. Speaking as a scholar he insisted that Jewish books must not be destroyed. They were valuable historical sources and important theological prooftexts. As such they must be preserved. 'The Jews,' he said, 'are our archivists, librarians, and antiquarians.'[8] Jewish exegetes, moreover, provided valuable philological explanations. Theologians who had attempted to interpret the Old Testament without a knowledge of Hebrew had committed laughable mistakes.

Reuchlin soon discovered that his opinion was the odd one out and that his critical remarks had made him unpopular with the theologians, not to speak of how it roused Pfefferkorn's ire. Pfefferkorn fought back with polemical tracts; the Cologne theologians took the procedural way. They instructed Arnold von Tungern, one of their faculty members, to examine the *Eye Mirror*, an annotated version of Reuchlin's report to the commission, for theological errors. On hearing of their manoeuvre, Reuchlin tried to forestall serious consequences. In a personal letter to Tungern he suggested that the faculty resented his report because he was not a professional theologian. He humbly acknowledged that he may have spoken out of turn and assured Tungern that he had meant no offence. Indeed he had the greatest respect for theology.[9] Unmoved by these explanations, the faculty censured the *Eye Mirror* for its 'Judaizing' content. The verdict of the Cologne theologians was confirmed by other universities, including the prestigious faculties of theology at Louvain and Paris, whose judgment was considered authoritative. Reuchlin's diplomacy effected only that the verdicts differentiated between the man and his book. They designated certain passages in the book as heretical, but did not accuse Reuchlin of being a heretic, since a heretic was by definition recalcitrant. The theologians of Erfurt, for example, insisted that the book must be 'suppressed, taken away, and destroyed,' notwithstanding that Reuchlin was a 'most learned man of singular and preeminent erudition, most knowledgable in the three languages, Hebrew, Greek, and Latin, and enjoying an excellent reputation for the integrity of his life and morals.' Similarly, the theologians of Mainz stated that they did not intend to injure 'the honour and reputation of the author, but after mature deliberation, decided unanimously that the said book should be removed for doctrinal reasons, that its use should be prohibited, and the book itself condemned.'[10]

The first official notice Reuchlin received from the Cologne theologians (January 1512) was restrained in tone. They attributed Reuchlin's 'errors' to ignorance and invited him to retract the *Eye Mirror* voluntarily. Reuchlin replied in the same tone that he had employed in his letter to Tungern, meekly acknowledging the 'scant resources of [his] mind' and his inability as a layman to understand the subtler points of theology.[11] He refused to recant, however, knowing that the verdict of the theologians by itself had no legal force. When the theologians opened court proceedings, Reuchlin's tone changed, prompting accusations of hypocrisy from Pfefferkorn.[12] The contrast between the humble letters he wrote to Tungern and the faculty between October 1511 and February 1512 and his *Defence against the Cologne Slanderers*, published a year later, was indeed striking and moved the controversy firmly into the realm of the humanist-scholastic debate.

The debate between humanists and scholastics began in fifteenth-century Italy as a literary polemic, but took on a different character when it reached Germany at the turn of the century.[13] There, the polemic was fought primarily in university circles where humanists and theologians were competing against each other. Whereas the focus of the earlier debate had been on the respective merits of philosophy and rhetoric and on the question of whether pagan writings were appropriate sources for a Christian scholar, the debate at German universities moved on to other issues. They ranged from mundane squabbles over salary and seating arrangements on official occasions to the question of competence and the right of humanists to comment on or apply textual criticism to scripture. In the rhetoric of the controversy, the theologians were typecast as inarticulate pettifoggers, whose only interest was logic and theology, and who regarded all other academic disciplines as inferior. Reuchlin's *Defence* contains all the commonplaces and catchphrases of the ongoing humanist-scholastic debate. He caustically noted that he had to lower his style to accommodate 'those trifling sophists.' He was using simple words so that his boorish adversaries could follow his arguments. He described logic as a subject fit for tyros and reproached the theologians for 'reverting to elementary things and, like boys, fooling around with syllogisms.' He accused them, moreover, of condemning other men's studies simply 'because they are not their studies and have not come from them. Like swine they delight in their own filth and tread on other scholars' pearls.'[14]

Two factors may explain Reuchlin's new aggressiveness. First, his earlier strategy had proved ineffective. His meek words failed to pacify the theologians since they were not accompanied by deeds, that is, compliance with their wishes. Secondly, Reuchlin no longer felt isolated, as he no doubt did on discovering that he was the lone dissenting member of the imperial commission. He was now receiving significant support from fellow humanists in the form of letters encouraging him to defend his position. In 1514 he published a selection of these letters, some of them fawning, under the title *Clarorum virorum epistolae* (Letters of Famous Men).[15] Pfefferkorn scoffed at the *Letters of Famous Men*. It was a backpatting exercise, he said. The humanists 'extol each other with mutual praise, rubbing each other's backs like porkers.'[16] It should be emphasized here that Reuchlin's champions supported his cause in so far as it was a humanist-scholastic polemic. Some of them pointedly separated the question of what to do with Jewish literature from the question of language studies, which was a specifically humanistic concern. The Nürnberg humanist Willibald Pirckheimer, a fellow jurist, assured Reuchlin of his support against the scholastics but regretted that he had engaged in controversy with Pfefferkorn, who had previously been 'unknown among learned men.' Similarly, Erasmus had no comment on the merit of Pfefferkorn's proposals or the contents of Reuchlin's report. He asked his patrons at the papal court to intercede for Reuchlin 'in the name of humanistic studies' and thanked them in advance for their 'great service to literature and all literary men.' The contents of Reuchlin's report and the arguments presented for and against it in court were 'a matter of no importance' to Erasmus, and 'going beyond even the ass's shadow of the proverbial jest.' He called Reuchlin's report 'a little book, a letter rather, and that written in German, which he never published himself nor intended for publication.' As far as he was concerned, Reuchlin's precious time was being wasted by involving him in litigation; he hoped that the intercession of his patron would restore Reuchlin to the world of learning.[17] Mutianus Rufus, the leading light of the circle of humanists in Erfurt and Gotha, had similar priorities. His position on the books of the Jews was in fact remarkably similar to those of Reuchlin's accusers. He asked Reuchlin 'not to favour the Jew, lest you harm the Christian.' He supported him as a humanist, however, because he saw Hoogstraten as an enemy of the *studia humanitatis*: 'In his monastery, he locked away all humanistic literature, threw it into the deepest dungeon so to speak, saying that "a man who loved the Muses had no [hope of] life and salvation."'[18]

From 1513 on, the controversy proceeded in two parallel strains, one using legal channels, the other working through a publicity campaign. The battle for public opinion was waged on Reuchlin's behalf by the humanistic party which included prominent writers like Erasmus and experienced publicists like Ulrich von Hutten. The Cologne theologians found willing mouthpieces in Pfefferkorn and in a younger member of the faculty of arts, Ortwin Gratius.[19] The legal battle was carried on by the inquisitor Jacob Hoogstraten in the twin roles of prosecutor and judge. It was based on the condemnation of the *Eye Mirror* by the Cologne theologians, who characterized the work as 'offensive to the pious ears of the faithful and especially to simple people, because it contains various articles that are doctrinally highly suspect and scandalous, smacking of heresy and agreeing very much with the perfidy of the Jews.'[20]

In September 1513 Hoogstraten cited Reuchlin before his court in Mainz, an invitation Reuchlin ignored. He knew that it was his right as a university professor to have the case dealt with directly by the papal court, and he made use of this privilege to escape from the jurisdiction of a man whose sympathies lay with the faculty of theology of which he was a member. On the direction of the papal court, the case was heard in the court of the archbishop of Speyer, where the climate was more favourable to Reuchlin and which had prominent humanists among the assessors and judges. Proceedings began in January 1514 and ended two months later with Hoogstraten's defeat. The judge imposed silence on him and held him responsible for the court costs. Hoogstraten had argued that Reuchlin was wrong to regard Jews as *concives*, fellow citizens; they were *servi*, servants of the empire. This was based on the conventional view that Christ's New Testament had superseded the Old Testament, that the Christian Church had defeated and subjugated the Synagogue. Hoogstraten insisted, moreover, that certain Jewish prayers were directed against Christians. This was the traditional medieval interpretation and had been adopted by Pfefferkorn in the *Enemy of the Jews*. In his report Reuchlin criticized this interpretation, rightly interpreting the prayers cited by Pfefferkorn as directed against a generic enemy. Elements of the humanist-scholastic debate made their way into Hoogstraten's charges as well. He pointedly denied that a knowledge of Hebrew was necessary for an understanding of the Old Testament and rejected out of hand Reuchlin's claims that medieval exegetes had made mistakes because of their unfamiliarity with classical languages. He denounced such criticism as offensive to the church. The central charge, however, was the accusation that Reuchlin's *Eye Mirror* was partial to Jewish exegesis, that is, it showed a Judaizing tendency. Hoogstraten did not accept his defeat at the hands of the Speyer judge and travelled to Rome to launch and personally pursue an appeal at the papal court. The theological faculty at Cologne continued to support Hoogstraten. They paid his expenses and were accused in humanistic circles of providing additional funds for the purpose of bribing the Roman judges.[21]

In response to the appeal, Pope Leo X formed a commission to investigate the case. While the commissioners deliberated, humanistically inclined churchmen such as the cardinals Adriano Castellesi and Egidio da Viterbo lobbied on Reuchlin's behalf. Hoogstraten was supported by his compatriot Adrian of Utrecht, a powerful man who was to succeed Leo as pope in 1522. In July 1516 the majority of the commissioners confirmed the Speyer judgment acquitting Reuchlin. Formally, however, the decision was in the pope's hands. In a diplomatic move, he suspended proceedings, thus depriving Reuchlin of a clear-cut victory, but also frustrating Hoogstraten, who remained in Rome for another year and finally returned to Cologne in the spring of 1517. The situation was generally interpreted as a moral victory for Reuchlin.

The polemic continued outside the courtroom, however. In his formal charges, Hoogstraten had alluded to the underlying debate concerning the merits of humanistic studies,[22] but an inquisitorial court was clearly not the appropriate stage to discuss such matters. Hoogstraten therefore addressed the subject in separate publications, in his *Apologia* addressed to Pope Leo X (1518) and again in the *Destructio Cabalae* (Destruction of the Cabala, 1519), a critique of Reuchlin's cabalistic studies. In the first tract he declared that the humanistic method was not suited to serious inquiries into the truth. Such an inquiry was 'difficult for a man who knows nothing but stories, who knows not a single proposition about ethics or things of the conscience, who does not know how to dispute in technical terms and keep to the point.'[23] The *Apologia* led to a polemic with Reuchlin's humanistic supporters. Hermann Buschius, Hutten, Pirckheimer, and Reuchlin himself replied (the latter anonymously). Buschius made fun of Hoogstraten's style. He was 'completely devoid of eloquence – why mention eloquence, when he is totally devoid of grammar? A seven-year-old boy would be ashamed to write like that to his teacher.' Hutten expressed the hope that the enemies of humanistic studies might soon perish.[24] Hoogstraten replied with an *Apologia Secunda* (A Second Apologia, 1519), to which Ortwin Gratius added a letter. The two men protested that the humanists were paying too much attention to form and not enough to content. Their infatuation with style blinded them to the message of the gospel which was expressed in humble language. 'They are nauseated by Christ's food,' Gratius wrote, 'so that they do not deign to see the fertile truth except when it is handed down with Ciceronian polish.'[25] Hoogstraten followed up with the *Destruction of the Cabala*, published the same year, in which he presented a more comprehensive defence of the scholastic method. It was the principal tool in the search for the doctrinal truth, he wrote. Aspects of the faith which were not explicit in scripture or the apostolic tradition depended on deductive reasoning, that is, on the use of the logical argumentation characteristic of scholastic theology. Hoogstraten's apologia constitutes a response to the humanists, who emphasized the philological over the logical method. An account of the court proceedings against Reuchlin, published by Ortwin Gratius and aimed at presenting the case from the theologians' point of view, also served to enhance Hoogstraten's position in the public eye and to counter humanistic propaganda.[26]

On the humanistic side, one of the earliest entries in the battle for public opinion comes from Crotus Rubeanus, a humanist from Erfurt. Crotus wrote a satire in response to the condemnation of Reuchlin's *Eye Mirror* by the theologians of Paris. The piece, entitled *Contra sentimentum Parrhisiense* (Against the Parisian Opinion, 1515), contains the record of a (fictitious) disputation between a jurist and a theologian concerning the faculty's condemnation of the *Eye Mirror* and concludes with an (equally fictitious) ecclesiastical verdict condemning the faculty. The disputation is cast as a humanist-scholastic debate, with the jurist 'Cutius Gloricianus' speaking on behalf of the humanists and the theologian 'Hackinetus Petitus' lamely arguing on behalf of the faculty. Gloricianus declares that the Parisians have condemned Reuchlin because they fear his influence: 'If he disseminates the literature and books of the Hebrews as he did earlier with Greek books and literature, he will through liberal studies draw away from them [the theologians] the majority of their students.' He alleged that the vote leading to the condemnation was rigged and the procedure flawed. Petitus conceded that the theologians 'greatly hate Reuchlin and the other champions of the humanities, and that they don't care for those poets,' but saw nothing wrong with that attitude. Similarly, he did not defend the voting procedures, but commented laconically that the faculty 'proceeded as they always do.'[27]

The most effective humanist defence of Reuchlin's cause was an anonymous satire entitled *Letters of Obscure Men*. This collection of fictitious letters was a group effort, with the main contributions coming from Ulrich von Hutten, at the time in the employ of the archbishop of Mainz, and Crotus Rubeanus. The authors lampooned Reuchlin's adversaries, depicting them in the stereotypical manner characteristic of the humanist-scholastic debate. The letters, all addressed to Ortwin Gratius,[28] are written in pidgin Latin and full of quibbles calculated to raise a laugh. The fictitious letter-writers mention the humanists with a hostility that is mingled with fear. They speak with nostalgia of the good old days when students devoted themselves to the study of logic and did not question the authority of their teachers. Now students preferred lectures on classical authors to the traditional curriculum and deserted their scholastic mentors. Since the study of literature did not prepare them for the baccalaureate, the number of students taking the examination declined. This affected not only the prestige but also the pocketbook of professors, since a part of their pay came from students' fees paid directly to the instructor and charges associated with examination and graduation. The letters reflected the competitive atmosphere at German universities. Although Pfefferkorn is frequently mentioned in the letters, the Jewish question is not central to the book and served only to ridicule the theologians who used Pfefferkorn in their battle against Reuchlin, although they could not shake off their prejudice against the converted Jew and suspected his personal integrity.[29] The most significant element in the *Letters of Obscure Men*, however, is the historical bridge built between Reuchlin and other humanists entangled in controversy with theologians. The ritualistic manner in which the same names are mentioned over and over again creates a canon of cases in the reader's mind and establishes a time line. Among the men whose polemics are frequently mentioned are Ulrich von Hutten, Hermann Buschius, Desiderius Erasmus, Willibald Pirckheimer, and of course Reuchlin, whose name is ubiquitous. Although these cases were complex and diverse, the satirists, using poetic licence, reduced them to disputes between humanists and theologians revolving around two issues: curricular and ecclesiastic reform. The accusations put into the mouths of the scholastic letter-writers were simplified correspondingly. They reviled the humanists as 'heretics' and rebels against authority. This characterization of the humanists as 'reformers' and challengers of the status quo facilitated the later crossover from the humanist-scholastic controversy to the Reformation debate.

A feeble attempt by Ortwin Gratius to respond in kind to the *Letters of Obscure Men* was unsuccessful. The leaden humour of his *Lamentations of Obscure Men* (1518) attracted few readers and had little impact compared with the *Letters of Obscure Men*, which turned into a bestseller and remained in print for the next four centuries. Reuchlin's court case, however, did not enjoy the same success. The affair, which after the adjournment of the case had continued as a polemic, became once more the focus of litigation when the condottiere Franz von Sickingen became involved in the case. Enlisted by Ulrich von Hutten, Sickingen interfered on Reuchlin's behalf, threatening the Dominican order with violence unless they put pressure on Hoogstraten to settle with Reuchlin. Sickingen, who was a law unto himself, had been placed under the ban, but when it became clear that the ban could not be enforced, the emperor found it more expedient to pardon Sickingen and make use of his services. Hutten, who was on friendly terms with the condottiere, interested him in Reuchlin's case. With the scholar's approval, Sickingen entered into negotiations with the Dominican order. The Dominicans temporized, signing an agreement with Sickingen, promising to withdraw their support from Hoogstraten and to urge Leo X to bring the court case to a conclusion 'without detriment to either party's reputation.'[30] In this manner the trial was resumed. The tide was running against Reuchlin, however. His affair was overshadowed by Rome's battle against Luther. In June 1520 Leo X signed the bull *Exsurge domine* which threatened Luther with excommunication. A few days later, Reuchlin's acquittal was overturned, and the *Eye Mirror* condemned. Hutten claimed in a letter that Reuchlin 'appealed,' but this could only be a figure of speech, for there was no higher instance than the papal court. It is unknown whether the judgment was enforced and Reuchlin was made to pay the fine. He died two years later, in 1522.[31] His name appears in the category of 'priests' in the lists of a prayer society, to which he belonged.[32] It is likely therefore that he was ordained shortly before his death, or even on his deathbed, a custom that served as a reaffirmation of one's beliefs and an expression of loyalty to the church.

By the time of his death, the Reuchlin affair had taken on mythical proportions. It was only fitting that Erasmus should compose an 'Apotheosis of Reuchlin' (1522), in which he described the scholar's entry into heaven. For humanists, Reuchlin had become a heroic figure. According to Erasmus, it remained only 'to inscribe the man's name in the calendar of saints.' In his eulogy, Erasmus unintentionally reinforced the connection between humanism and the reform of the church. He depicted Reuchlin not only as a humanist through whom God 'had renewed the gift of the three languages' but also as a reformer who would 'confound the speech of the pseudoapostles plotting ... to obscure his glory.'[33] Presumably he meant the scholastic theologians who had attacked Reuchlin, but the word 'pseudoapostles' was also part of the polemical rhetoric of the Lutherans, whose movement was now threatening the unity of the church.

CHAPTER 3

# Reuchlin and the Luther Affair

The *Letters of Obscure Men* provided a first conduit for the idea that the Reuchlin affair had been an overture to the Reformation controversy. In the 1520s, several of the humanists active on Reuchlin's behalf had become associated with Luther. Erasmus, Pirckheimer, Buschius, and Hutten had been mentioned repeatedly in the *Letters*. Soon after their publication, 'Erasmus laid the egg, and Luther hatched it,' became a popular witticism. Pirckheimer's name had been appended to the papal bull condemning Luther, formally identifying him as one of the reformer's adherents. Buschius had turned provocateur, openly defying church law by taking part in a meal featuring dishes of meat during Lent. Hutten was one of the most aggressive promoters of the Reformation, engaging in terrorist-style attacks on the Catholic clergy and encouraging Sickingen to declare war on the church. These developments led to a reinterpretation of the Reuchlin affair. The *Letters of Obscure Men* merely implied a link between Reuchlin and Luther; the private correspondence of their contemporaries soon made this link explicit. Christoph Scheurl, legal advisor to the city of Nürnberg, was among those who made the connection, warning Luther's opponents that they would be challenged in turn, not only by the followers of Luther but also by 'all Reuchlinists.'[1] Willibald Pirckheimer placed Reuchlin in a line-up together with Luther, Erasmus, and the French biblical humanist Jacques Lefèvre, depicting all four as victims of the scholastic theologians.[2] The Swiss humanist Melchior Vadianus likewise grouped Reuchlin together with Erasmus and Luther, explaining that they were attacked by the theologians 'because they speak rather freely.'[3] Such testimonies were reinforced by pictorial representations.

Crotus Rubeanus, rector of the University of Erfurt, had an illustration inserted in the register of the university that linked Reuchlin with Luther. It showed an arrangement in which the rector's crest was surrounded by images of Luther, Erasmus, Reuchlin, Hutten, and a number of Erfurt humanists. Similarly, a Strasbourg pamphlet shows Reuchlin, Hutten, and Luther together under a banner proclaiming them 'patrons of liberty.'[4]

Luther himself took an early interest in Reuchlin's case, focusing his attention on the issue of censorship. In Luther's time, certain restrictions were generally accepted, among them, the rule that non-theologians must not dispute matters of faith. Luther was incensed, however, that even opinions that did not concern articles of faith were subjected to censorship and denounced as heretical.[5] He did not entirely share Reuchlin's appreciation of Jewish literature, but he was determined to defend his academic freedom to pursue Hebrew studies. Later, when he drew parallels between his own case and those of Reuchlin, Pico della Mirandola, Valla, and Erasmus, he was referring to censorship as a common threat. However, the names he cited had until then been invoked as champions of humanism and served as examples of the humanist-scholastic debate. Luther was transferring them to a new context, blending the academic with the theological controversy. In his *Resolutions of the Disputation Concerning the Efficacy of Indulgences* (1518) he drew attention to the earlier cases: 'Note what happened to Giovanni Pico della Mirandola, Lorenzo Valla, Peter of Ravenna, and ... most recently Johannes Reuchlin and Jacques Lefèvre: contrary to their intentions, their well meant words were perverted and made out to be evil.'[6] We find a similar grouping of cases in his *Response to the Doctrinal Condemnation by the Louvain and Cologne Theologians* (1520).[7] Once again he referred to Pico della Mirandola, Valla, Reuchlin, Erasmus, and Lefèvre, this time explicitly linking his case with Reuchlin's. The theologians of Cologne had lost their case against Reuchlin, he said, and were now casting around for another victim. They had seized on Luther, hoping to triumph in his case and recoup their earlier losses.

In these polemical statements, Luther places himself in the same circle of men mentioned earlier on by Reuchlin and the authors of the *Letters of Obscure Men*. In the original setting, the names were invoked to create a feeling of solidarity among humanists, to establish a historical pattern of humanists being attacked by scholastic theologians, and to cast Reuchlin as a typical example of such confrontations. Did Luther's case fit the description as well? Not in the eyes of Erasmus, who bluntly said that humanists had no good reason to engage themselves on behalf of Luther as they had done on behalf of Reuchlin: 'After all, Luther is not so far advanced in the knowledge of the tongues or of elegant scholarship to provide supporters of such studies with an interest in his case.'[8] Erasmus's reaction shows that Luther, by drawing on the same historical examples as the authors of the *Letters of Obscure Men*, suggested to readers that his polemic was part of the humanist-scholastic debate. From our vantage point we can see that he was a theologian battling against theologians, but Luther's contemporaries were less certain about how to categorize him. In the early stages of the Reformation, Luther is repeatedly mentioned in the same breath with Erasmus, implying that both men were advancing humanistic studies and were victimized by scholastic theologians for that reason. Mutianus Rufus, for example, called Erasmus the inspirational source of men like Oecolampadius, Philip Melanchthon, and Martin Luther, all of whom were in his eyes 'leading men of letters.' Similarly, Claude Dieudonne linked Luther with Erasmus and Reuchlin, calling their enemies 'persecutors of good literature'; a letter from the Literary Society of Selestat likewise connected Erasmus with Luther, referring to the two men as 'leaders of *studia meliora*,' that is, of humanistic studies.[9] Agrippa of Nettesheim connected the judgment which the Cologne and Louvain theologians had passed on Reuchlin's report with their condemnation of Luther's Ninety-five Theses. 'What reputation have you gained as a result of fighting Reuchlin?' he asked the theologians rhetorically. 'What advantage did you get from going against Erasmus of Rotterdam, Lefèvre d'Etaples, and Peter of Ravenna?' Similarly, they had gained no advantage from proceeding against Luther. They had merely effected that 'the Lutheran affair grew from a spark into an immense conflagration.'[10] The parallel is obvious: Just as Reuchlin and his supporters had placed his case in the context of a larger controversy between the champions of the New Learning and the scholastic theologians, Luther and his champions portrayed the hostilities he suffered at the hands of Catholic theologians as part of a larger pattern. Their efforts contributed to the confusion prevailing in the early 1520s over the relationship between humanism and the Reformation. The idea that the New Learning had 'caused' the schism remained an idée fixe in the writings of radical Catholic theologians long after it had become clear to more thoughtful minds that humanists and reformers pursued essentially different goals.

CHAPTER 4

# Sixteenth-Century Interpretations of the Reuchlin Affair: Beliefs or Constructs?

Sixteenth-century writers offer a variety of interpretations of the Reuchlin affair, but are they spontaneous expressions of opinion or artificial constructs serving a strategic purpose? In its first stages, the Reuchlin affair was depicted as a campaign against Judaism. This interpretation was promoted by Pfefferkorn; it also forms the basis of Hoogstraten's indictment and of the condemnations of Reuchlin's *Eye Mirror* by a number of universities. This corporate understanding of the Reuchlin affair reflects the pervasive Christian bias of European society at the time. The same bias provided the rationalization for the wars against the Ottoman Turks, the subjugation of American natives, the expulsion of Jews and Muslims, and the numerous inquisitorial proceedings guarding and enforcing Christian doctrine, morality, and practices. In that sense the Reuchlin affair was business as usual and constitutes the unexamined and unreflective perpetuation of long-standing traditions. For Pfefferkorn, however, the battle against non-Christian values was not a tradition 'sucked ... into the bottom of our hearts, even with our mother's milk,' as Tyndale put it.[1] It was not the result of unremarked cultural assimilation to which every member of a given society is subject. On the contrary, it constituted a break with his native tradition and a conscious adoption of alien values. Indeed, Pfefferkorn's emphasis on the anti-Judaic angle of his conflict with Reuchlin serves a personal goal: it supports his efforts to refashion his persona and prove himself a genuine Christian. In adopting a polemical stance, he displays an attitude characteristic of the convert struggling to establish his new identity. His life was a 'life lived as a project,' as Stephen Greenblatt says in *Renaissance Self-Fashioning*.[2]

Pfefferkorn's effort to redefine himself and realign his loyalties became an all consuming task, executed with zeal and fervour. Many of the features Greenblatt describes in his analysis of Tyndale's confessional change or 'refashioning' of the self recur and are applicable to Pfefferkorn: the rage against the old authority; the rejection of old practices as wrong and delusory; the 'intense need for something external to himself in which he could totally merge his identity,' which explains why the old authority must immediately be replaced with a new one.[3] Refashioning himself becomes a preoccupation with Pfefferkorn so that it is not surprising to find several of his tracts beginning with a reference to his new identity: 'I, Johann Pfefferkorn, once a Jew but now a Christian, have composed this booklet in praise of God and his hallowed Mother, for the benefit of the common weal, and for my own salvation.'[4] Without accusing Pfefferkorn of being a poseur and falsely advertising his conversion, we observe a certain self-referential purpose in his writings. His interpretation of the Reuchlin affair as a crusade against Jews and a showdown between orthodox Christians like himself and a Judaizer like Reuchlin, satisfied a deeper personal need. It provided Pfefferkorn with a mission that transcended the personal cause of defending himself against Reuchlin's charges of ignorance and lifted the polemic above the level of a vendetta into the more lofty sphere of a fight about principles.

The second interpretation which places the affair in the context of the humanist-scholastic debate makes its first covert appearance in Reuchlin's report, as we have seen. The characteristic arguments and catchphrases he uses there signal to the alert reader his membership in the humanistic party. They include an emphasis on the propaedeutic value of language studies for theologians, on examining the biblical texts in the original languages, and on the legitimacy of consulting non-Christian sources. Reuchlin pointed out that the church fathers had no scruples reading non-Christian authors. He justified his philological interest in the Hebrew and Greek texts of scripture, defending them against the charge that they were 'false.' Arguing as an experienced textual critic, he notes that even the Latin Vulgate, which was regarded as authoritative by the theologians, could be called 'false' in the sense that all manuscripts and printed copies were subject to corruption by inattentive scribes and print-setters. He cites St Jerome as a witness: 'With so many translators and interpreters working on it, it is no wonder that the text has been signally corrupted and contains many errors, as Saint Jerome notes and writes.' Insisting on the importance of going back to the original text, he recommends the hiring of two lecturers in Hebrew at every German university. A knowledge of Hebrew, he added, could also serve missionary purposes.[5] He had urged theologians to study Hebrew in an earlier work as well. Using the catchphrases of the humanist-scholastic debate, he recommended the study of Hebrew in *The Wonder-Working Word* (1484) and complained that theologians 'paid more attention to the dialectical sophisms of Aristotle than to the divinely inspired words of the Holy Spirit.'[6] Finally, Reuchlin's commitment to humanism is made explicit and expressed in an aggressive and polemical tone in his *Defence against the Cologne Slanderers* (1513), as we have seen.

Turning to the question of whether Reuchlin pursued a strategic aim in depicting his case as a humanist-scholastic debate, that is, that he wanted to attract a following among humanists, we observe that he expressed his allegiance to the humanistic cause prior to his entanglement with Hoogstraten and the theologians of Cologne. It would appear therefore that Reuchlin did not deliberately construct a humanistic platform to attract followers among the humanists. One might say, however, that he availed himself of the circumstances, welcomed the support of like-minded scholars, and made skilful use of the print medium to publicize it.

Reuchlin had good reason to fear the charge of anti-Judaism and thus an incentive to shift the focus of the debate. The researches that had made him a paragon in the eyes of humanists also made him vulnerable to charges of Judaism. His *Rudiments of Hebrew* (1506), a combination of grammar and lexicon, contained criticism of the traditional Vulgate text, which was bound to raise the hackles of scholastic theologians. He had noted discrepancies between the Hebrew text and the Vulgate translation, declared that the translation was inferior, the translator 'dreaming' or 'blathering.'[7] In many cases he suggested improvements that were not merely idiomatic, but changed the meaning.[8] In the preface, he expressed the hope that theologians might learn from him, a suggestion that invited trouble, for professional theologians did not look kindly on what they regarded as meddling in their business by unqualified persons.[9] By engaging in scriptural studies, Reuchlin was therefore entering dangerous territory. In 1512 he published a translation and interpretation of seven psalms,[10] in which he kept mostly to philological points, but often diverged from the normative Vulgate translation and occasionally criticized the exegete Nicolaus of Lyra, who was regarded as authoritative by scholastic theologians.[11] His work would certainly have been regarded as trespassing by the theologians. Two generations earlier, the Italian humanist Lorenzo

Valla had been severely criticized for attempts similar to Reuchlin's. His collation of Greek and Latin manuscripts of the Gospels and his observations on the discrepancies were regarded as unwarranted interference in matters that concerned only theologians. Valla escaped an inquisition into the orthodoxy of his writings only because he enjoyed the protection of the Neapolitan court. His case was by no means an isolated one. In Spain the manuscripts of the philologist Elio Nebrija were confiscated by the Inquisitor because they touched on biblical names. In France, Jacques Lefèvre, by profession a teacher of philosophy, had published biblical commentaries and translations. Soon accusations of heterodoxy were brought against him by the theologians of Paris, who drove him into exile. Similarly, Erasmus's efforts to collate Greek and Latin manuscripts of the New Testament were disparaged by the theologians of Louvain, and the finished work, a bilingual, annotated, edition of the New Testament (1516), involved him in numerous controversies as well as inquisitorial proceedings in Spain and France. Each one of these men was rebuked by theologians for 'putting his sickle into another man's crop,' a phrase taken from canon law and denoting interference with another man's jurisdiction. Like Reuchlin, Erasmus insisted on the strictly philological nature of his enterprise. Theologians, however, rightly observed that changing the words often changed the meaning as well. In other words, when philology was applied to scriptural texts, the task of the grammarian could not be neatly separated from that of the theological exegete. The explanation that humanists were engaging in scriptural studies in the capacity of philologists did not satisfy them.

It is with some justification, therefore, that Reuchlin saw himself as the latest victim of scholastic theologians battling humanists. Valla, Nebrija, Lefèvre, and Erasmus had been attacked for their Greek studies; Reuchlin, who engaged in the study of Greek and Hebrew, the mother tongue of the 'murderers' of Jesus, faced additional hazards. His position was suspect even though he had taken a conservative attitude toward Jews, repeating the commonplace argument that they were suffering for the sins of their fathers and even using derogatory language in his polemic against the 'Taufjud' Pfefferkorn.[12] In the public eye, his actions were not unequivocal. He cultivated friendly relations with Jewish scholars. He had defended the Jews in his report to the imperial commission, not only as *concives*, fellow citizens, but also as fellow human beings deserving of Christian love. In his *Defence* he had noted that one should use caution in conversations with Jews, but one must treat them with *caritas*, Christian love, and must not deny them *quod ius humanae societatis concedit*, what is theirs by the right of human society.[13] His defence of the Talmud was risky, moreover, since the book had been condemned repeatedly and its possession outlawed, although the prohibition does not seem to have been enforced, as demonstrated by the need for renewing the pertinent legislation. Reuchlin himself had to admit the questionable nature of some Hebrew works, for example, the notorious *Nizzachon* (Victory). Yet, by 1514, Reuchlin owned manuscript copies of both the Talmud and the *Nizzachon*.[14] His interest in the Jewish cabala was likewise bound to involve him in controversy.

The publication of *The Cabalistic Art* in 1517, at a time when the controversy with the theologians was by no means over and which goaded Hoogstraten into a published response, suggests that Reuchlin had not deliberately sought to deflect attention from his alleged Judaism by shifting the affair to new ground. He maintained his interest in Hebrew writings and made no effort to conceal it. It would appear therefore that Reuchlin's depiction of the affair as a humanist-scholastic debate did not serve the strategic purpose of ingratiating him with German humanists or shift the centre of the accusations. Indeed, he had proclaimed his support for humanism much earlier, when it served no strategic purpose and exposed him to the ill will of conservative theologians, and he continued to pursue humanistic studies, including Hebrew, when it was counterproductive to achieving a settlement. We should, however, distinguish purpose from outcome. While Reuchlin may not have purposely depicted the affair as a scholarly concern, he may have found it convenient to allow this interpretation. Perhaps he preferred being labelled a 'theologizing humanist'[15] to being labelled a Judaist. At the time, it may have seemed the less dangerous charge, although none of the biblical humanists of Reuchlin's generation escaped harassment and censure.

We now turn to the third interpretation, which links Reuchlin with Luther. In this case we have evidence of a strategic purpose behind the interpretation. It was, if not artificially created, certainly artificially maintained. This suggestion goes back to the sixteenth century itself. Erasmus suggested in 1520 that the confusion between humanism and the Reformation was encouraged by interested parties. He himself believed that the Reuchlin affair was an aspect of the humanist-scholastic debate and that linking Reuchlin with Luther was detrimental to the humanistic cause. Humanism, he correctly predicted, would be made a scapegoat by theologians battling the reformer. He therefore made a concerted effort to disentangle the two movements. 'What have the humanities in common with the business of faith?' he asked. In his opinion the concept, or rather the misconception, that humanism and the Reformation shared a common platform may have arisen spontaneously but was now perpetuated by the protagonists for reasons of their own. Humanism was popular with the young generation, and the reformers attempted to 'captivate the minds of the young people with their professed interest in languages and literature.'[16] There is some evidence for Erasmus's conspiracy theory. Several leading reformers, Melanchthon, Bucer, and Zwingli among them, were all at one stage under the impression that Erasmus was one of them and were hoping that he, as the leading humanist, would deliver that party to them. In 1519, for example, Melanchthon spoke of Luther as 'our foremost champion, second only to Erasmus'; similarly, Bucer wrote in 1518 that 'Luther agrees in everything with Erasmus, with the only difference that what Erasmus merely hints at, Luther teaches openly and freely.' Both men revised their opinion in the 1520s. Bucer saw the light in 1524 when Luther and Erasmus engaged in a published controversy over free will; Melanchthon declared already in 1522 that Luther was committed to 'true, evangelical, Christian preaching' whereas Erasmus merely taught 'good manners and civility.' In other words, Luther was a reformer, Erasmus merely a humanist. The printer Ulrich Hugwald sums up the situation when he states that anyone still under the impression 'that Luther or any other evangelical has anything to do with [Erasmus], whom people once raised up to heaven for his achievements,' had no understanding of true religion.[17] Hugwald's 1522 comment suggests that an intelligent observer would be able to tell that the aims of humanists and reformers were not interchangeable; that humanism could be compatible with church reform, but was not necessarily so. Although the distinct nature of the two movements was becoming increasingly obvious and cracks were developing in the relationship between the leading men, there appears to have been an interest in certain circles to maintain a united front in public. Hutten, for example, was quite candid about the strategic importance of such a move. In a letter to Erasmus, he noted that some people regarded Erasmus as Luther's inspirational source. 'You were the forerunner, you taught us, they say ... you are the man on whom the rest of us depends.' Of course this was not true, Hutten said. Nevertheless he pleaded with Erasmus to conceal his disagreement with Luther. It was in the interest of humanists to keep a common front with the reformers, he said. A successful Reformation movement guaranteed that 'liberal studies too will flourish and the humanities will be held in honour.' Luther himself wrote to Erasmus in a similar vein: 'If you cannot or dare not be assertive in our cause, leave it alone and keep to your own business.' To a fellow reformer (Oecolampadius) he wrote: 'I feel Erasmus's barbs occasionally, but since he pretends in public not to be my enemy, I in turn pretend that I do not understand his clever words.'[18] There is some evidence, then, supporting the allegation that the reformers encouraged for some time the idea that they had much in common with the humanists, and specifically that Reuchlin's case was a harbinger of the controversies between Catholic theologians and reformers. The strategic importance of keeping a common front prompted them to maintain the construct of a joint mission long after it had become clear that the two movements represented different currents of thought.

## CHAPTER 5

# The Reuchlin Affair in Modern Historiography

The complexities of interpreting the Reuchlin affair are apparent in modern historiography as well. We have seen that Reuchlin was variously portrayed as a Judaizer, a humanist, or a pre-Reformer. All three interpretations have left their imprint on modern historiography. In the nineteenth century and up to the Second World War historians tended to emphasize the humanist-scholastic angle over other aspects of the Reuchlin case. Ludwig Geiger's biography, *Johann Reuchlin: Sein Leben und seine Werke* (Leipzig, 1871), which remains the classic account today, represents this tendency. Geiger acknowledged that the affair began as a crusade against the Jews, but regarded the confrontation between humanists and scholastics as the principal feature. By 1511, he said, 'the business of the [Jewish] books was over,' and the intellectual battle began. 'It had its origin in the battle over the books, to be sure, but ... its character changed forthwith and assumed an essentially different form. There were barely any references to the books from that point on, and none at all to the Jews. At issue was the right to express one's opinion freely, to counter the inquisitorial fixation on heresy' (240). According to Geiger, the Reuchlin affair galvanized the nascent movement of northern humanism: 'As humanism began to increase in vigour, as people began to rid themselves of the chains of ignorance, kindred minds who were as yet few in number and barely conscious of their own power and uncertain of their inherent strength, felt a need to band together' (367). The Reuchlin case provided the external stimulus. The humanists came to recognize their common interests: 'If one of them was attacked, they must all join in his defence' (323). Geiger's interpretation remained prevalent until the first half of the twentieth century. Thus Carl Krause in his life of the humanist Helius Eobanus Hessus stated that the affair was a struggle between barbarism and learning that 'threatened the principle of humanism.' Similarly Paul Joachimsen in an article on the development of humanism wrote that the question of the Jewish books was unimportant in comparison with the battle between humanism and the 'party of scholastic monks.'[1]

This is not to say that historians of the nineteenth century completely passed over the anti-Judaic angle of the Reuchlin affair. As is to be expected, the issue takes centre stage in Heinrich Graetz's monumental *Geschichte der Juden* (Leipzig 1852–76). Although Graetz entitled the pertinent chapter 'The Feud between Reuchlin and Pfefferkorn or The Talmud as Shibboleth of Humanists and Obscurantists,' he had little to say about the latter subject and concentrated on the anti-Semitism of Pfefferkorn and his supporters. He saw the affair as a polemic between Pfefferkorn, 'an ignorant, thoroughly vile creature, the scum of the Jewish people ... a dung beatle' and Reuchlin, a man 'of pure, upright character, nobility of mind, integrity which was proof against temptation, admirable love of truth, and a soft heart.' Graetz acknowledged that Reuchlin 'at first' shared in the anti-Judaism characteristic of his time, but insisted that ultimately 'his heart did not share the prejudices of his head.'[2]

It may be pertinent to mention here that both Geiger and Graetz were ethnic Jews, since Julius Schoeps recently raised the question whether there was a discernable Jewish point of view ('eine spezifisch jüdische Sichtweise') in accounts of the Reuchlin affair.[3] Focusing his attention on Graetz, Geiger, and Guido Kisch (*Zasius und Reuchlin*, Constance, 1961), Schoeps comes to the conclusion that the affair did indeed attract the special attention of authors of Jewish descent but that there was sufficient variety and nuancing in their accounts to discount the idea of a link between ethnicity and point of view. Clearly, ideology or Zeitgeist were more important markers than biographical factors. A chronological division of accounts therefore casts more light on historiographical trends than a division by the authors' ethnic origins. The 1940s certainly form a dividing line. The issue of anti-Judaism, or more specifically anti-Semitism, was given greater weight after the Second World War. In the wake of the Holocaust and the crimes perpetrated by the Nazi regime, we find a greater sensitivity to the issue of anti-Semitism. Racial discrimination and, more generally, ethnocentricity, were targeted not only at the philosophical level but also at the level of popular liberal thought. This change in habits of thought is evident in historiography as well. Heiko

Oberman in his examination *The Roots of Antisemitism* has noted that the battle over Jewish books and its anti-Semitic undertones gained new significance in postwar accounts of the Reuchlin affair.[4] Indeed, Guido Kisch expressly recommended studying the Reuchlin affair from this angle. Hitler's anti-Semitism would not have found such fertile ground, he said, if it had not been ideologically prepared in the preceding centuries. Important historical lessons could be drawn from the Reuchlin affair. An essay by Wilhelm Maurer, published in 1953, likewise exemplifies the new sensitivity. He expressed regret that Reuchlin's role in the history of Jewish emancipation had been underestimated in the past.[5] These are also James Overfield's priorities. In his monograph on *Humanism and Scholasticism in Late Medieval Germany* he provides this overall assessment: 'Of course it would be foolish to argue that tension between humanism and scholasticism played no part in making the Reuchlin affair the long and acrid controversy that it was. But ... the status of the Jews and their books was a more important issue than the status of humanism and scholasticism.'[6]

Max Brod's *Johann Reuchlin und sein Kampf* (Stuttgart, 1965) also bears the stamp of post-war thinking. Brod's original plan was to write a historical novel but, as he explained in an interview: 'First I thought of describing Reuchlin's life and significance in a novel, but I was so captivated by the subject that I decided to write a historical work that strives for the greatest possible degree of objectivity in portraying Reuchlin.' Margarita Pazi, who examined Brod's writings, notes that he shows a greater willingness to speak his mind and take a personal stand in the Reuchlin book than he does in his other writings. It is characteristic of Brod's accounts of intellectual battles to give each side its due, but history had 'sharpened his awareness of the danger inherent in allowing issues to remain unresolved.' In what sense, then, was he 'objective'? Brod felt called upon to take an unequivocal position on the Reuchlin affair without, however, manifesting the partisan spirit of Graetz, whose black and white account he found 'instinktlos' (insensitive).[7] Indeed, Brod is representative of a trend that has taken shape in the last thirty years: he strives for a more balanced and nuanced account of the Reuchlin affair. Kisch, for example, acknowledged the importance of Reuchlin's stand in the history of Jewish emancipation; at the same time, however, he recognized the polemic as a humanist-scholastic controversy, a 'battle between the spirit of a rising humanism and a calcified old scholasticism tied to traditions.' In his view, the accounts of Graetz and Geiger were the products of 'sentimental optimism' that made Reuchlin the hero of a cause championed by the authors.[8]

In recent years, Heiko Oberman has argued for a more balanced approach. He notes with approval that the Reuchlin controversy was no longer interpreted 'as a "titanic" struggle between humanism and scholasticism.' 'This is definitely an improvement,' he comments. At the same time he believes that Reuchlin's own interpretation should not be overlooked. And for Reuchlin humanism was an important issue in the controversy.[9] Oberman therefore warns of privileging one interpretation over the other in the absolute terms used, for example, by Johannes Helmrath, who said that the 'attacks of Reuchlin's opponents from Cologne and of others ... were essentially motivated by antijudaism, not by antihumanism.'[10] Stephan Rhein in a recent essay made the same point when he criticized Erdmann-Pandzic for privileging the issue of anti-Semitism and saying that 'even at the beginning of the dispute the anti-Semitic motive was so preponderant that the issue of the Jewish books was merely derivative and can hardly be regarded as an independent issue per se.'[11] In a similar vein, Hans Peterse, whose monograph *Jacob Hoogstraeten gegen Johannes Reuchlin* is the most recent book-length contribution, praises a nuanced approach that gives due consideration to the diverse factors shaping the controversy and expresses regret that such an approach has not yet been universally adopted.[12]

Most modern accounts, then, concentrate on the anti-Judaic and/or antischolastic aspects of the Reuchlin affair. The third interpretation current in the sixteenth century – Reuchlin as pre-Reformation figure – is largely absent. Hans Hillerbrand is one of the few scholars to discuss Reuchlin's 'legacy' to the Reformation. Although he speaks of a 'reworking' of Reuchlin's ideas, he proclaims valid the 'lapidary assertion that a Reformation without Reuchlin is unthinkable,' if only because he 'liberated scholarship.'[13] In speaking of a 'lapidary assertion,' Hillerbrand presumably thought of Graetz, who stated that the controversy 'aroused German consciousness and created a public opinion without which the Reformation ... perhaps would never have been born at all.'[14] However, most scholars today join Oberman in describing this interpretation as outdated or discredited.[15] Max Brod relates with a mixture of humour and frustration an experience during a visit to Reuchlin's grave in 1962: 'As you enter [St Leonard's in Stuttgart], the church custodian presses on you a cellophane-wrapped piece of cardboard with historical explanations. Some of the information is incorrect or at any rate correct only in a very qualified sense, for example: "Beside the pillar next to the altar lies buried the famous humanist Johannes Reuchlin. He was a forerunner of the Reformation ..." Forerunner? Reuchlin, who in the last years of his life was ordained priest!' Brod points out that this interpretation had been wishful thinking on the part of those who championed the Reformation in the sixteenth century and who would have liked to see a common front between all those who had experienced the censorious hand of the university theologians. 'They overlooked in this that the partisans of humanism and the Reformation had already begun to feel a mutual antagonism.'[16]

Although the link between Reuchlin and the Reformation is an implausible historical construct, it has a place in historical accounts of the Reuchlin affair. The epistemological doubt that has induced historians to question the possibility of value-free narration and the realization that they will always reflect the cultural assumptions of the narrator, has also led to a greater willingness to let alternatives stand side by side. Indeed it has become a more important task to examine how events were perceived than to establish 'how things actually happened.'[17]

# Notes

## Chapter 1: Pfefferkorn and the Battle against Judaism

1 I am using the comprehensive term 'anti-Judaism' to describe sixteenth-century attitudes toward Jews. The term includes (1) anti-Semitism, that is, hatred of the Jews as a group that was culturally and ethnically distinct from the majority; (2) religious discrimination, that is, the condemnation of the Jewish religion which, according to Christian theologians, denied the 'Christian truth' and the prosecution of 'Judaizers,' that is, persons favouring Jewish teaching and practices, whether or not they were ethnic Jews (Reuchlin being an example of a non-Jew); and (3) the rejection of 'Jews' in a metaphorical sense, that is, Christians taking a legalistic approach to religious observances, which in the sixteenth century was identified with Old Testament practices and therefore labelled 'Jewish.' The Reuchlin affair illustrates anti-Judaism in the first two senses of the word. Cf. G. Langmuir, *Toward a Definition of Antisemitism* (Berkeley, 1990), 311–52.

2 The content of the pamphlet is reprinted in H.-M. Kirn, *Das Bild vom Juden im Deutschland des frühen 16. Jahrhunderts* (Tübingen, 1989), 179–80.

3 E. Böcking, ed., *Ulrichi Hutteni Equitis Operum Supplementum* (Leipzig, 1864), I: 164.

4 See below, Document 6, and Pfefferkorn's denial, Böcking, *Supplementum*, I: 170.

5 Böcking, *Supplementum*, I: 84, 172.

6 Ibid.

7 For the most recent detailed biographical account, see Kirn *Das Bild*, 9–12.

8 Böcking *Supplementum*, I: 145.

9 *Defence against the Cologne slanderers*, A iv verso, B ii recto.
10 Böcking, *Supplementum*, I: 145.
11 A short tract, entitled *In Praise and Honour of the Emperor* (1510) contains a preface by an otherwise unknown Andreas Kanter informing the reader that he undertook the translation from German into Latin at Pfefferkorn's request (D2 verso).
12 Böcking, *Supplementum*, I: 175.
13 Ibid., 158.
14 Viktor von Karben, *De vita et moribus Iudeorum* (Paris, 1511), 65 verso.
15 For a recent detailed account of the economic conditions of German Jews, see R. Overdick, *Die rechtliche und wirtschaftliche Stellung der Juden in Südwestdeutschland im 15. und 16. Jahrhundert* (Constance, 1965); R. Po-chia Hsia and H. Lehmann, eds., *In and Out of the Ghetto: Gentile-Jewish Relations in Late Medieval and Early Modern Germany* (New York, 1995); H. Oberman, *The Roots of Anti-Semitism in the Age of Renaissance and Reformation* (Philadelphia, 1984); A. Herzig, 'Die Juden in Deutschland zur Zeit Reuchlins,' in A. Herzig and J. Schoeps, eds., *Reuchlin und die Juden* (Sigmaringen, 1993), 11–20; G. Kisch, *The Jews in Medieval Germany: A Study of Their Legal and Social Status* (Chicago, 1949).
16 On such superstitions and their fatal consequences for Jewish communities see R. Po-Chia Hsia, *Trent 1475: Stories of a Ritual Murder Trial* (New Haven, 1992). On being asked about such practices, Pfefferkorn declared that he had never heard of such crimes being perpetrated and offered the plausible explanation that such rumours might have arisen out of a misinterpretation of Passover ceremonies. He did not defend the Jews, however, adding: 'I know nothing further about these things; I only know that they plot many other evil and most cruel things against the Christians every day' (Böcking, *Supplementum*, I: 86). On the Jews in late medieval Germany more generally, cf. A. Foa, *The Jews of Europe after the Black Death* (Berkeley, 2000), and K. Stow, *Alienated Minority: The Jews of Medieval Latin Europe* (Cambridge, MA, 1992).
17 *Collected Works of Erasmus* (*CWE*) Ep. 1006: 149–50
18 See below, Document 9.
19 Böcking, *Supplementum*, I: 173.
20 In another booklet on the art of preaching (*Liber congestorum de arte praedicandi*, 1502) he provides as a sample sermon a homily against the Jews.
21 *Martin Luthers Werke: Kritische Gesamtausgabe* (Weimar, 1883–) 11: 314–15 (cited hereafter as *WA*). The tract created positive responses among some Jews, but they were based on a misunderstanding. Thus, Rabbi Abraham ben Elieser Halevy hailed Luther as a destroyer of Christianity. Cf. M. Awerbuch, 'Über Juden und Judentum,' in Herzig and Schoeps, *Reuchlin und die Juden*, 198.

The literature on Luther's attitude toward the Jews is vast. For a good summary and bibliography see M.U. Edwards, 'Against the Jews,' chapter 6 of *Luther's Last Battles: Politics and Polemics, 1531–46* (Ithaca, 1983); and M. Brecht, *The Preservation of the Church*, vol. 3, *Martin Luther*, trans. J. Schaaf (Philadelphia, 1985). Cf. also H.H. Ben-Sasson, 'Jewish-Christian Disputation in the Setting of Humanism and Reformation in the German Empire,' *Harvard Theological Review* 59 (1966), 369–90.

22 In 1515 Charles asked the pope to pronounce against Reuchlin's book, which 'in many passages openly helped and favoured the Jews' (Böcking, *Supplementum*, I:150). On the disputation in 1530, see E. Opitz, 'Johann Reuchlin und Josel von Rosheim,' in Herzig and Schoeps, *Reuchlin und die Juden*, 105–6.

23 *Ich bin ain Buchleinn der Juden veindt ist mein namen* (Augsburg, 1509), translated into Latin by an unidentified translator under the title *Hostis Iudeorum hic liber inscribitur*, with a prefatory poem by Ortwin Gratius (Cologne, 1509). For selections from this pamphlet, see below, Document 1.

24 *Enemy of the Jews*, 1509, c ii verso.

25 Ibidem, b i recto; the account of the debt accumulating over thirty years is given on b i verso – b ii recto.

26 Ibid.

27 The pamphlet was first published in German, then translated into Latin. The German text has been published as an appendix in Kirn, *Das Bild*, 205–30. The passage quoted appears there on 225.

28 *Jewish Confession*, A ii recto, B ii verso.

29 Ibid., B iii recto

30 Böcking, *Supplementum*, I: 85.

31 Writing to the archbishop in November 1509, Maximilian explained that he had mandated Pfefferkorn to 'make visitations, examine and look at all books and writings of the Jews and to take away and suppress any books he found offensive to the Christian faith.' He was to act 'with the consensus and counsel and provident care of the [local] priest, two [city] council members, or at any rate on their authority' (Böcking, *Supplementum*, I: 89).

32 Ibidem. In the meantime, however, Pfefferkorn, who had begun to confiscate books in Frankfurt, continued his campaign in Worms, Mainz, and other German cities.

33 Ibid., 83, 103, 102, 114, 120.

34 Ibid., 95 (from the report of the University of Cologne).

35 Ibid., 106.

36 Ibid., 91; I. Kracauer, 'Actenstücke zur Geschichte der Confiscation der hebräischen Schriften in Frankfurt a. M.,' *Monatsschrift für Geschichte der Wissenschaft des Judentums* 44 (1900), 126, 224, 173. Cf. D. Andernacht,

*Regesten zur Geschichte der Juden in der Reichsstadt Frankfurt am Main von 1401–1519* (Hannover, 1996).

37 Böcking, *Supplementum*, I:109. The proverb is quoted in Latin, 'doctrina facit perversos'; the German is 'die Gelehrten, die Verkehrten.'

38 Ibid., 111.

39 Ibid., 91, 101.

40 Ibid., 114.

41 Ibid., 170.

**Chapter 2: Reuchlin and the Scholastic Theologians**

1 Reuchlin gave Loans an honourable mention in the Hebrew grammar he published in 1506, calling him a man 'most learned in my opinion' and a 'most humane instructor' (quoted by Geiger, *Johann Reuchlin*, 106 n. 3).

2 The duke expelled the Jews from Tübingen in the same year in which he founded the university (1477); in his will he forbade Jews to reside or trade in Würtemberg (1492).

3 On Question 5, quoted by Geiger, *Johann Reuchlin*, 169 n. 4. For the Christian involvement in cabalistic studies, see J. Leon Blau, *The Christian Interpretation of the Cabala in the Renaissance* (Port Washington, 1965); F. Secret, *Les Kabbalistes chrétiens de la Renaissance* (Neuilly, 1985); P. Beitchman, *Alchemy of the Word: Cabala of the Renaissance* (Albany, 1998); C. Wirszubski, *Pico della Mirandola's Encounter with Jewish Mysticism* (Cambridge, MA, 1989); J. Dan, ed., *The Christian Kabbalah: Jewish Mystical Books and Their Christian Interpreters: A Symposium* (Cambridge, MA, 1997); C. Zika, *Reuchlin und die okkulte Tradition der Renaissance* (Sigmaringen, 1998).

4 Letter to Arnold of Tungern, 1511, Böcking *Supplementum*, I: 117.

5 *Johannes Reuchlin: Gutachten über das jüdische Schrifttum*, ed. A. Leinz-Dessauer (Stuttgart, 1965), 84 ('They are of the opinion that their faith is the right one, and ours wrong'), 86 ('They contend that Jesus is not divine, and everything that follows from that we must accept as being their faith'). Cf also *Eye Mirror* (*Johann Reuchlin: Sämtliche Werke*, IV–1, 132): 'But this is certainly incorrect: that they exceed the limits set by their own faith and blaspheme Christ and our faith in the books in which they defend and corroborate their faith.' An English translation of the report appeared while this book was in preparation: P. Wortsman, ed., *Recommendation Whether to Confiscate, Destroy and Burn All Jewish Books: A Classic Treatise Against Anti-Semitism*, with introduction by E. Carlebach (New York, 2000).

6 See below, p. 90.

7 In his *Defence against the Cologne Slanderers* (*Reuchlin: Werke*, IV–1, 340, 346) Reuchlin says: 'We must treat them with charity,' 'They are human beings and our brothers.'
8 See below, p. 94.
9 Böcking, *Supplementum*, I: 117.
10 Ibid., 136–8.
11 Ibid., 131.
12 Reuchlin, he said, was 'at variance with himself and inconstant'; his 'falsity and feigned compliments' had been of no avail, however (ibid., 119, 143).
13 On this subject, see E. Rummel, *The Humanist-Scholastic Debate in the Renaissance and Reformation* (Cambridge, MA, 1995).
14 *Defensio* C 1 recto. The theme appears also in a letter to Frederick of Sachsen, May 1518 (Geiger, *Johann Reuchlin*, Ep. 256): 'The sophists have made fools of us with their useless blather, not without harming the church; we were unable to understand the wisdom of old because of our deficiency in Latin, Greek, and Hebrew.'
15 Tübingen, 1514; followed by *Illustrium virorum epistolae* (Letters of Illustrious Men, Hagenau, 1519).
16 Böcking, *Supplementum*, I :157
17 *CWE*, Ep. 333: 113, 116, 132–3, and Ep. 334 in Document 9, below.
18 *Mutianus Rufus: Briefwechsel*, ed. C. Krause, in *Zeitschrift des Vereins für hessische Geschichte und Landeskunde* (1885), Supplement IX, 353, 434.
19 Ortwin Gratius (d. 1542) was a member of the faculty of arts at the University of Cologne and worked for the press of Quentel as a proofreader. In 1514 he published an account of the trial, *Historica et vera enarratio iuridici processus habiti in Maguntia* (A History and True Account of the Trial Held in Mainz). Cf. Peterse, *Jacobus Hoegstraeten*, 35.
20 Böcking, *Supplementum*, I: 135.
21 See Peterse, *Jacobus Hoegstraeten*, 56.
22 Published in 1518 under the title *Libellus Accusatorius … contra Oculare Speculum* (Book of Accusations against the *Eye Mirror*).
23 *Apologia*, a4 recto–verso
24 The letters of Buschius, Hutten, and Reuchlin were published in *Epistolae trium illustrium virorum* (Letters of Three Illustrious Men, 1519), cf. Peterse, *Jacobus Hoegstraeten*, 87–91. The quotation is on 88 n. 73.
25 *Apologia secunda*, A6r.
26 See above, n. 16.
27 Böcking, *Supplementum*, I: 319–21
28 Gratius was singled out because he regarded himself and was seen by others as a humanist. See Hutten's poem, *Reuchlin's Triumph*: 'You brag

in public that you are a poet' (Böcking, *Supplementum*, III: 433, lines 581–2). The humanist party regarded his collaboration with the Cologne theologians as a betrayal.

29 See the selection of texts in Document 5.

30 Quoted by Peterse, *Jacobus Hoegstraeten*, 136

31 A surprising number of reference works give incorrect information on this point. The 1997 *Encyclopedia Britannica* article on Reuchlin says that in 1516 a papal commission acquitted Reuchlin of heresy. Apart from obscuring the fact that Reuchlin ultimately lost his case, the account concludes enigmatically that his stand 'had proven beneficial to the Protestant cause' (vol. 10, p. 4). The 1996 German *Brockhaus* accurately states that Reuchlin, although supported by humanists, suffered defeat in court, but incorrectly asserts that the affair ended in 1511, almost a decade before the papal court rendered its verdict (vol. 18, p. 307). The *Encyclopedia of the Renaissance*, ed. T. Bergin and J. Speake, a reference work published in 1987, declares that the pope 'quashed' the court case in 1516 and that Reuchlin 'spent his last years quietly teaching and studying' (344).

32 Cf. H. Decker-Hauff, 'Bausteine zur Reuchlin-Biographie,' in M. Krebs, ed., *Johannes Reuchlin 1455–1522* (Pforzheim, 1955), 83–107.

33 The 'Apotheosis' was published in Erasmus's *Colloquies* (*Opera omnia Des. Erasmi Roterodami* [Amsterdam, 1969–] I–3, 274–5), hereafter cited as *ASD*.

**Chapter 3: Reuchlin and the Luther Affair**

1 *Scheurls Briefbuch*, ed. F. von Soden and J. Schnaake (Potsdam, 1867–72), Epistle 192.

2 *Opera*, ed. M. Goldast (Frankfurt, 1610, repr. Hildesheim, 1969), 374.

3 Melchior was the brother of the Swiss reformer Joachim Vadianus. The quotation comes from *Die Vadianische Briefsammlung* (St Gallen, 1894), II: 264.

4 Illustration in H. Weissenborn, *Acten der Erfurter Universität* (Halle, 1884), II: 152; J. Benzing, *Bibliographie der Schriften Johannes Reuchlins im 15. und 16. Jahrhundert* (Vienna, 1955), Illustration 1. See also below, chapter 5, n. 10.

5 *WA*, *Briefe* I, Ep. 7.

6 *WA* I: 574; see below, Document 13.

7 See below, Document 13.

8 *CWE*, Ep. 1167: 113–14.

9 Mutianus Rufus, *Briefwechsel*, Ep. 634; A.-L. Herminjard, ed., *Correspondance des Réformateurs dans les pays de langue française* (Geneva, 1866–97)

I: 72–3; A. Horawitz and K. Hartfelder, eds., *Der Briefwechsel des Beatus Rhenanus* (Leipzig, 1886), 221.

10 *Apologia adversus calumnias* (Cologne, 1533), C vii recto.

**Chapter 4: Sixteenth-Century Interpretations of the Reuchlin Affair**

1 Quoted by S. Greenblatt, *Renaissance Self-Fashioning* (Chicago, 1980), 88.

2 Ibid., 107

3 Ibid., 85, 90, 111.

4 *Enemy of the Jews*, a i verso.

5 *Report* (Reuchlin, *Gutachten*, ed. A. Leinz-v. Dessauer) 71, 73, 89, 91, 105. See also below, Document 4.

6 *De verbo mirifico*, ed. W.W. Ehlers et al. (Stuttgart, 1996), 192.

7 *Rudiments*, 523 (nescio quid blacterat); 571 (ubi nescio quid nostra translatio somniavit).

8 Geiger, *Johann Reuchlin*, 122 n. 3, gives a list.

9 Reuchlin, *Briefsammlung*, 7 March 1506.

10 *In septem psalmos poenitentiales hebraicos interpretatio de verbo ad verbum et super eisdem commentarioli sui ad discendum linguam hebraicam* (A literal translation and short commentary on the seven penitential psalms in Hebrew, for the student of the Hebrew language), Tübingen, 1512.

11 'I am surprised that Lyra did not see this when he laboured over the literal meaning' (*Psalmi*, k4 a).

12 He accuses the 'baptized Jew Pfefferkorn' (taufft Jud) of seeking revenge, thus falling back on his old Jewish nature (*Eye Mirror* in *Reuchlin: Werke*, IV–1, 152).

13 *Defense* in *Reuchlin: Werke*, IV–1, 340.

14 Cf. illustration in *Reuchlin: Gutachten*, ed. Leinz-v. Dessauer, 109, showing that a copy of the *Nizzachon* had been given to Reuchlin by Johann Dalberg, bishop of Worms, in 1494; he acquired a manuscript of the tract 'Sanhedrin' (part of the Talmud) in 1512 (see illustration ibid., 108). For a modern edition and translation of the *Nizzachon*, cf. D. Berger, ed. and trans., *Nizzahon: The Jewish-Christian Debate in the High Middle Ages: A Critical Edition of the Nizzahon Vetus* (Northvale, 1996).

15 An expression coined by the Paris theologian Noël Beda to denote the trespassing philologists.

16 *CWE* Ep. 1033: 228–9; *Opus epistolarum Des. Erasmi Roterodami*, ed. P.S. Allen (Oxford, 1906–58), Ep. 1690: 66–7 (hereafter cited as 'Allen').

17 *Melanchthons Briefwechsel*, ed. H. Scheible (Stuttgart, 1977), I: 49; Bucer in *Briefwechsel des Beatus Rhenanus*, ed. A. Horawitz and K. Hartfelder

(Leipzig, 1886), 107; *Corpus Reformatorum*, ed. C.G. Bretschneider and H.E. Bindseil (Halle, 1834–60), XX, 701; *Correspondance de Martin Bucer*, ed. C. Krieger and J. Rott (Leiden, 1995), I, Ep. 13; Hugwald in *Die Vadianische Briefsammlung*, 246.

18 *CWE* Ep. 1161: 18–21, 46–7 and Ep. 1135: 48–9; *WA* Br III 96.

**Chapter 5: The Reuchlin Affair in Modern Historiography**

1 C. Krause, *Helius Eobanus Hessus: sein Leben und seine Werke* (Gotha, 1879), 167–8; P. Joachimsen, 'Der Humanismus und die Entwicklung des deutschen Geistes,' *Deutsche Vierteljahrsschrift für Litteraturwissenschaft und Geistesgeschichte* 8 (1980), 460–1.

2 The quotations come from the English translation of the work: *History of the Jews* (Philadelphia, 1894), IV: 423, 432–3, 435.

3 J. Schoeps, 'Der Reuchlin-Pfefferkorn-Streit in der jüdischen Historiographie des 19. und 20. Jahrhunderts,' in A. Herzig and J. Schoeps, eds., *Reuchlin und die Juden* (Sigmaringen, 1993), 203.

4 'The battle for the rights of the Jews has gained a significance that it did not have for Reuchlin to this extent' ('Johannes Reuchlin: Von Judenknechten zu Judenrechten,' in Herzig and Schoeps, *Reuchlin und die Juden*, 41)

5 W. Maurer, 'Reuchlin und das Judentum,' in E.-W. Kohls and G. Müller, eds., *Kirche und Geschichte: Gesammelte Aufsätze* (Göttingen, 1970), II 333–46.

6 James Overfield, *Humanism and Scholasticism in Late Medieval Germany* (Princeton, 1984), 253.

7 M. Pazi, 'Max Brod über Reuchlin,' in Herzig and Schoeps, *Reuchlin und die Juden*, 214; Max Brod quoted ibid.

8 Quoted ibid. 210, 211.

9 H. Oberman, 'Johannes Reuchlin: Von Judenknechten zu Judenrechten,' in Herzig and Schoeps, *Reuchlin und die Juden*, 54–5.

10 Johannes Helmrath, 'Humanismus und Scholastik und die deutschen Universitäten um 1500: Bemerkungen zu einigen Forschungsproblemen,' in *Zeitschrift für Historische Forschung* 15 (1988), 187–203; Helmrath's remark is quoted by Oberman, 54.

11 Stephan Rhein, 'Reuchliana III. Ergänzungen,' in *Johann Reuchlin (1455–1522)*, ed. H. Kling and St. Rhein (Sigmaringen, 1994), 303–25 on E. von Erdmann-Pandzic and B. Pandzic, *Eine Untersuchung zum Kampf für die jüdischen Bücher mit einem Nachdruck der 'Defensio praestantissimi viri Joannis Reuchlin' (1517) von Georgius Benignus* (Bamberg, 1989), 70.

12 Peterse, in a historiographical survey in the introduction to his book, 15.

13 Oberman, 54; Hillerbrand, in 'Vom geistigen Holocaust zur rechtlichen Toleranz: Bemerkungen zum Thema Johannes Reuchlin und die Reformation,' in Herzig and Schoeps, *Reuchlin und die Juden*, 110, 113. He cites the title page of the German pamphlet *History Von den fier ketzeren Prediger ordens* of 1521, in which Reuchlin, Hutten, and Luther are described as 'patroni libertatis' (patrons of freedom), a term laden with significance that would have been associated with Luther's *Liberty of the Christian* published the previous year. Hillerbrand, rather ahistorically, connects this with modern liberation theology ('wir würden heute sagen: Befreiungstheologen,' 114).

14 Graetz, *History of the Jews*, 423 (similar, 467), 461.

15 'Heute ist die Verkoppelung Reuchlins mit der Reformation theologiegeschichtlich diskreditiert' (Oberman, *Reports*, 39). He notes that the chronological coincidence of their controversies meant that the Reuchlin affair necessarily continued after 1517 under different connotations (54).

16 M. Brod, *Johann Reuchlin und sein Kampf* (Stuttgart, 1965), 342, 20.

17 As the goal of historical investigation was famously designated by L. Ranke, *The Theory and Practice of History*, ed. G. Iggers and K. von Moltke (Indianapolis, 1973), 137.

# Part B

# TEXTS

## DOCUMENT 1

# Johann Pfefferkorn

# *The Enemy of the Jews*

The following translation is based on the German edition published in January 1509 by the Augsburg printer Erhard Öglein (a2recto–c3verso). An expanded Latin version appeared two months later from the press of Heinrich von Neuss in Cologne. The most significant differences between the two versions have been indicated in the notes. Pfefferkorn's German reflects everyday usage and contains patterns that are typical of oral delivery. It lacks refinement and is occasionally awkward. The transliteration of the Hebrew phrases mirrors local dialect and the Hebrew itself contains mistakes, some of which could, however, have been introduced by the printer.[1] On the whole, the Latin version, whose author is unknown, is more hostile toward the Jews than the original (see, for example, notes 2, 3, 15, 28, 41, 42). It is not clear to what extent Pfefferkorn himself suggested or approved of the changes. The translator occasionally substitutes precise theological language for Pfefferkorn's general terms (see, for example, note 11); more often he clarifies expressions that are unidiomatic or colloquial. The Hebrew is much improved in the Latin version.

### *The Enemy of the Jews*

In praise of God and his blessed mother. To promote the common good and also to save myself, I, Johannes Pfefferkorn, once a Jew but now a Christian, have produced this booklet and divided it into three parts: In the first I will tell of various insults and shameless words the Jews[2] utter every day against God, Mary his most worthy mother, and the whole heavenly host; and I will offer proof in their Hebrew language.

In the second part I will tell of and explain the harm and damage the Jews cause to the country and the people through usury, as you will hear. In the third part I shall note how they incite Christians with whom they share living space to commit ungodly and unchristian acts through their illgotten wealth, which they spend lavishly in the interest of their affairs. I shall end by telling how they are plotting to murder and destroy me (as I clearly report and have been loyally warned of). I do so[3] in hopes that Christian leaders will take my words to heart and ponder and prevent the damage which the mangy dogs do to Christian power in both the spiritual and the worldly sphere.

The first part of this booklet tells of the disrespect and the blasphemies of the Jews uttered every day against God, Mary his blessed mother, and the whole heavenly host.[4]

First, the faithless Jews do not allow the sweet name of Jesus and, equally, of Mary to pass their poisonous lips nor do they wish to pronounce them. Our saviour, in particular, has among them three disrespectful and horrible names. The first is 'Jescheynozere,' נוֹעְרִי יֵשֶׁ, that is, a seducer of the people;[5] the second is 'tholin,' תָלוּי, hung;[6] the third is 'mamser ben hanido,' חֲנִדָה בֶן מַמְזֵר, one born from an unclean union.[7] In this way the noble Son of God is every day slandered by the rascals and ridiculed in a blasphemous manner.

In the same way, Mary the noble Mother of God, is also called by three disrespectful and shameful names. The first is 'thlüa,' תְלוּיָה, the female hangman;[8] the second is 'sono,' זוֹנָה, a notorious sinner;[9] thirdly she is called 'thmea,' טְמֵאָה, one who lives uncleanly. And when the Ave Maria bells are tolled in the mornings and evenings, according to the Christian rite, the Jews say: that is the bell of the female hangman, 'thlüa,' תְלוּיָה. In the same way, they call Our Dear Lady's Day 'thlüa,' יוֹם תְלוּיָה, the day of the female hangman.[10]

In the same way, the holy, most worthy sacrament, the body of Christ,[11] is likewise called and termed in horrible fashion 'lechem-thome,' טָמֵה לֶחֶם, the unclean bread. And when the holy body of Christ is brought to someone, they say one did or wants to 'methame,' מְטַמֵּה, that is, to make someone unclean.

In the same way, our Christian priests are called in their language 'gallehim,' גַלֵּיחִם, shorn ones.[12]

Item, the chalices are called 'clavim,' כְּלָבִים, so many dogs.

Item, they call the churches 'mosschoff,' or 'beskisse,' 'כִּסֵּה בֵּת מָשׁוֹב, that is, [latrines or] shithouses.[13]

Item, they call the apostles or young Christians 'tschmidem,' תַשְׁמִידִם, exterminators.[14]

Item, the Latin language is called in Hebrew 'laschanthome,' טוּמְּה לָשׁוֹן, unclean tongue.

Item, they hate the sign of the holy cross and find it quite unbearable. If they see pieces of wood or straw on the ground that are by chance arranged roughly in the shape of a cross, they push it apart with their feet that they may no longer have to look at it.[15]

Item, no Jew knowingly crosses a churchyard or listens to an organ. If it happens, however, he believes that his prayers will not be heard by God for thirty days.

Item, they have two special prayers against us Christians ... [The first runs:] 'There is no hope for the baptized, and all infidels will soon be gone and all the enemies of your people Israel will be suppressed and destroyed. This will happen soon.'[16] They pray these words every day three times with great devotion. [The words] at the beginning denote the holy apostles and their successors, who received baptism and who do not observe their false beliefs, and whom they regard as infidels. They also pray for vengeance against the whole Christian church and especially the Roman Empire, that it may be broken up and destroyed. And they are not allowed to say this prayer sitting down; rather, they must stand. Nor are they permitted to talk among themselves until the prayer is ended. And if war or rebellion breaks out among us Christians, they are heartily pleased, hoping that the time is near when the Empire[17] will be destroyed.

The second prayer is said on their long day, when they confess to the roosters[18] and believe that they are quite cleansed of sins, and it runs: ...[19] 'May God destroy the thoughts and counsel of our enemies with death, sword, starvation, plague, and other scourges, and may it happen for our sake.'[20] All these words are spoken against us Christians. There is no denying. If the Jews falsely argue that the Christians are not their enemies, I reply: they hate the Christians much more than other nations, and if they act friendly toward us Christians, it does not come from the heart. They act in this way because we Christians believe in Jesus Christ and regard him as the Messiah, which goes entirely against them.

Item, if a Christian comes to a Jew, he receives him and says: Seind wilkum, meaning 'Devil, be welcome,' for seth means devil.[21] And although they sometimes offer us a drink, after we have drunk, no Jew uses the cup again, unless it has been washed three or four times.[22] And as I said earlier in my booklet, they confess to a rooster, but sometimes it happens that some of them cannot obtain a rooster because they are poor or for some other reason. In that case, they stand by their door in the morning and remain there until they see a Christian. Then they say secretly to the Christian: You will be my capon this year and die an evil death for my sins.

And this is the end of the first part of the booklet.[23]

The second part tells how the Jews corrupt the country and the people. Although one encounters many sects and creeds in the world, there is among all of them none more thieving, swindling, and more harmful to Christendom than the unclean and cursed sect of the Jews, who more than any other nation always, day and night, earnestly ponder and zealously plot how to uproot the power and might of Christians and destroy them. Since, however, they are unable to accomplish this, they use usury and other kinds of deception (as I shall show in due course), hoping to be successful through friendly words, and affable manners and gestures.

Attend me kindly so that you may note and recognize their skill. You know that they lend money against a pawn which must always be worth more than the sum they are asked to lend. And therefore, when someone comes to a Jew with an article to be pawned, the Jew knows that that person is under duress. Yet he addresses the Christian with friendly words, inquiring after his wishes. Then the Christian says: 'I have here an article which I would like to pawn for such and such a sum of money.' Then the Jew takes the pawn, inspects it all round and replies: 'Indeed, I cannot lend that much in return for it'; and he pretends that he does not want to lend him anything. The Christian is intimidated because he needs the money, and he says to the Jew: 'What and how much, then, will you lend me?' Then the Jew turns the pawn back and forth once again, inspecting it closely, and after a long examination, he says: 'A ring, of all things!' And he names a small sum he is willing to lend on, say, a ring. For example, he is willing to lend one gold Gulden ... And although the Christian needs more money, he takes the Gulden, hoping soon to redeem his pawn. In the meantime the Christian becomes poorer by the day (for I know for sure: anyone who falls in with the Jews and does business with them will never flourish) and cannot redeem his pawn. Yet he keeps hoping for an improvement. And when one year is over and past and the Christian does not redeem his pawn, which is worth much more than the loan, it has passed by default to the Jew for the small sum that he lent for it, and he does not return it once the year has passed. If, however, the Christian comes before the year is over, say on the last day of the year, and settles his account with the Jew, 34 Cologne Weisspfennig and 8 Heller are due on the gold Gulden.[24] The Christian cannot pay and begs the Jew to let the interest accrue together with the initial loan at the usual rate. Then the Jew replies: 'With pleasure, but you need to bring me more collateral.' And that is what the Christian does. He allows the interest to be added to the Gulden, hoping that his affairs will soon improve, but this does not come to pass. As I said before: the deeper a man becomes involved with the Jews, the less he can get away from them, and so the second year passes and the Christian comes once again to settle his account with the Jew. And now the sum owed by the Christian to the Jew for the second year on the original loan plus the interest amounts to 2 Gulden and 46 Weisspfennig and 4 Heller. The Christian finds out the amount and cannot pay it. He begs the Jew, as before, to let the interest accrue together with the original loan. The Jew agrees to this, but says that he must bring him more collateral. The Christian has to comply. If he does not, the Jew takes the pawn into the city and publicly offers it for sale. Thus the Christian is embarrassed before a number of people, and so the Christian brings everything he has in his house and privately hands it over to the Jew. Now that the Jew has for one Gulden goods valued at a hundred Gulden or more, the poor Christian has nothing left to pawn and runs away and must live in poverty for the rest of his life. This happens a great deal and often ...[25]

Now someone may say: My dear man, there is no one who will leave a debt of a Gulden stand for such a long time and accumulate so much interest on it. I would like to answer him: Even if the said Gulden happens to be paid back and the pawn is redeemed in the first year or at any other time, that same Gulden and interest is that same hour lent to someone else who pays the usurious interest. For the Jews find people enough and in sufficient numbers, who run after them day and night to borrow money. They charge usurious interest not just to one sinner and on one Gulden but on many, which comes to a significant sum over thirty or a hundred years. For there are many places where the Jews have lived for a hundred years, and during those years they have lent a huge, significant, remarkable, and unbelievable sum of Gulden. Through such usury they have amassed a remarkable profit, sucked from the poor people. This I have set down here fairly, as you can see.

Item, consider in the name of God and think what a treasure the rascals collect. So much money falls into the Jews' hands without work, through usury alone, especially money that accrues to them from stolen goods and plunder that remains in their hands. Also from what they steal themselves, which they do freely without compunction. If a Jew steals jewellery worth ten thousand Gulden and it is found at his place, he says it was given him as collateral for such and such a sum. And they believe him, and he is reimbursed for the sum lent.[26] In this business, then, they are more privileged than Christians. If one were to find stolen goods or other suspect wares in a Christian's house, they would be taken from him without compensation[27] and, in addition, they would drag the man by his neck and throw him into prison and interrogate him under torture[28] to discover where these goods came from. Because the dogs have been granted such privileges, they rightly laugh at Christians. From these words of mine every prudent man may see the remarkable extent to which Christian power is weakened and reduced by the Jews' evil wiles.

Item, usually if a Christian is involved in a lawsuit with a Jew concerning a pawn or a similar matter, the Jew is allowed to swear a Jewish oath,[29] on account of which the Christian is deprived of his jewellery or wares which he has acquired with difficulty and hard work. And the Jew is willing to do this, although he knows very well that he is wrong, and he does not listen to his conscience but swears a false oath against the Christian. And if a Jew refuses the oath and does not want to swear it, he does this not out of fear of God or for the sake of the truth, but out of human concern that his own authorities might hear of the false oath. For this reason no one should think that the oath of a Jew against a Christian is trustworthy ...

Whence comes[30] our simple-mindedness and excessive credulity approaching blindness in the face of their snares, if one may say so, that we not only commit and entrust our business to Jews to our great detriment, but even our bodies and lives? Many Jews, even the most unlearned (note the audacity of their race and their fraudulence) profess to have medical knowledge. And they show medications to Christians or offer their services without being asked and sometimes bribe Christians who may have been cured by them to make known and to praise their knowledge in the presence of others. Many of the Jews who vaunt their knowledge and boldly practice medicine are certainly ignorant of medicine. I admit that there are some among the Jews who know a great deal about medicine who have handed on the proofs of their learning to posterity in books, like Rabbi Moses and Isaac and any others that the Jews may have among them now[31] ... [They lack the theoretical foundation, however.] They have no knowledge of physics, no understanding pertaining to natural science. Without distinguishing between diseases, without inquiring into their causes, without taking notice of the circumstances, they boldly and daringly promise good health, selling medicine and giving out whatever they may first glimpse in a book. And their comments make no allowance for place, time, age, complexion or diet and other matters which a physician should most diligently consider. They, by contrast, want to cure everyone's eyes with one salve, as the proverb says, and men who have never studied medicine dare to promise everything, boasting of their knowledge of this art, while they have not touched on even its basic principles. In my view (pardon me) it appears not at all reasonable that a Christian should entrust his life and safety to a Jew, first of all to an ignorant person who is his natural enemy, and especially when there is among Christians such an abundance of physicians who know the theory which supports and underpins this art, who, after giving consideration to theory, finally have come to practise the art in a manner that is rational rather than haphazard. But what can be more absurd than a Christian entrusting his physical safety to a Jew rather than to a Christian? Unless, perhaps, someone says: What difference is there between physicians? There is a great difference between a learned and an unlearned man, an experienced and inexperienced man, a compatriot or a stranger, a friend or an enemy, whether you entrust yourself to chance or to skill. For example, when Ochozia, king of Israel, was ill and consulted foreign gods (for the physician is like a god), he was advised not to ask false and erroneous gods, as we read at 4 Reg 1 [2 Kings 1]. When Ochozia, son of Achab, king of Israel, was ill, he sent messengers to Beelzebub, the principal god of the Achari – what hope of safety did he have? Heli intervened and ordered the messengers to return. He said to the king: 'Why have you sent messengers to Beelzebub, the god of the Achari? As if there were no god in Israel from whom you could make inquiry?' He warned him: 'Therefore, oh Lord, you will not recover from this illness but die.' That is exactly what it means to abandon Christian physicians, who are learned in theory and versed in practice and speak the truth, and to turn to unlearned and inexperienced Jews.

The third and last part tells how the Jews, through their ill-gotten wealth, cause Christians to commit great sins.

Wherever Jews live, one must worry about them using their wealth to lead astray not only the common people but even educated men, insofar as the latter help them to cover up their injustice. For even if a Jew has to answer with his life and body, people can be found who will give him aid and succour, contrary to the commandment of the Christian church. It is obvious in the case of several villages and cities where Jews live that they usually prevail in court and quite rarely lose their case. The only reason for this is their ill-gotten money, which Christians accept from them in exchange for helping to muddle and cover up their case and make it appear just.[32] For this reason some Christians are deprived of justice, insofar as more concessions are made to the Jews than to the Christians. Furthermore, the Jews cause many Christians, learned and unlearned, to doubt their faith, as I have shown in other books of mine. Thus there is much heresy where Jews live; also one finds that Christians commit unchaste acts with Jews and have children by them. These children remain Jews, which is no doubt a great, notable, and shameful evil. Christian blood is subjected to eternal damnation and, as I have mentioned at the beginning of my booklet, there is in the whole city no sect or nation that hates the Christians more than the Jews; and they hate me especially and other men also who were once Jews, more than they hate other Christians; and I know well, if I fell among Jews, they would devour me as the wolf devours sheep, for this was reported to me. I was warned secretly by a good friend, who informed me in writing that Jews from several countries have made a pact to kill and murder me. But to assure that they would escape punishment after killing me, they prompted several false Christians to speak of me and say: 'Yes, Pfefferkorn is a fellow whom one must not believe. He makes you Christians believe whatever he wants, as long as he gets money from you, but when he has filled his pockets to his heart's desire, he will at an opportune moment suddenly decamp. Then it will become apparent what kind of man he is.'

Therefore I beg all Christian believers[33] to listen kindly to my words. The Jews talk of me in this manner only for this reason: to cover up their deed if I am sooner or later killed and murdered secretly by the allies of the Jews,[34] and to be able to say: 'See, now you discover that we told you the truth. We knew he wouldn't stay but would run away, as we said earlier on.' Oh, you devout Christians, if I should disappear, have no other thoughts than that I was killed by the Jews as they killed others before me. Oh heavenly God, why should I desire to pass once more from light to darkness? For if I regard the books of Moses together with the prophets and the law of nature itself and all life on earth, I find by right and well-considered reason that the Jews are walking in darkness; and I shall demonstrate this clearly and briefly with some passages drawn from Holy Writ. In addition I shall show with modest words the central hope of the Jews. They await a Messiah who will deliver them. They think he will come as a secular ruler, a king with great power and wealth to rule and subdue the world ...[35]

They likewise hope devoutly that the temple [in Jerusalem] will be rebuilt.[36] Then they would with great piety have their priests sacrifice calves, lambs, sheep, steers, rams, and doves, in praise of the living God and the cleansing of their sins, as was done in the Old Testament. To this I reply: ...[37] From the prophecy [of Isaiah and Jeremiah] one may see that God is no longer willing to accept the sacrifices of the rejected Jews, and that the Jews meet only with disdain in God's eyes and are regarded as sinners, and that their rituals must no longer be honoured and enforced ... When their priests sacrifice the above mentioned lambs and steers in the temple and I or another person were to be present and to say prayers, God would pay little attention, at least according to my understanding. In my opinion their temple is a butcher shop rather than a house of God.[38] I also think that their priests are butchers ... If God were pleased with them, they would have been heard long ago and delivered from their misery. Yet even in former days they often attracted God's great wrath because of their idolatry and their murder of prophets, but when they called to God, they were delivered from captivity. But now God will no longer save them or hear their prayer, for they have committed greater sins than their forefathers, who have killed the prophets. They have killed the Son of God. That is why I will never commit myself to them again. A second reason why I have separated from the unclean race is this:

When I thought about the great number of Christian churches that have people of such manifold and great learning and, likewise, their praiseworthy laws, and if after such thoughts I should fall in once more with the Jews, I would be a greater fool than our first father Adam, when he ate the apple contrary to the commandment of God, following the counsel of the devil's serpent.[39]

Item, when I mentioned in the first part of this booklet the insulting language used by the damned Jews against our Lord Jesus, Mary, the sainted apostles, and the whole host of the holy Christian church, the blasphemy and filth they utter against the divine truth, someone may say that even if it is true I should have spoken more discreetly. To avoid giving offence to anyone, I should have used different words and spoken prudently and not expressed myself in such rough and rude terms. To that person I reply, giving him two reasons that rightly moved me. First, I have revealed things that have long been hidden and have now been brought to light in their own Hebrew language and script and translated into German.[40] But if the German were different and not in accord with the Hebrew letters, the Jews might have an excuse and say: 'Pfefferkorn writes a great deal in our Hebrew script, but that is not the truth.' And they might punish me for my words, for the Jews are used to interpreting all scripture literally.

Secondly I ask on behalf of all Christians who read or hear this, to take it to heart, and resist the perverse race with all the more determination, and to despise them;[41] and I wrote this especially for Christians who are in contact with Jews, so that they may be enlightened and come to the right insight, and when this happens – and even if only one among them all is moved by my writings, I have gained a brother.

Thus I want to end my booklet. If, however, someone is moved in his heart by this and wants to prevent the blasphemy of God uttered by the Jews every day, I would like to reply and say: as long as the Jews live freely, it is not possible to avoid such evil. For it would not be enough for them to abandon usury and go on living in great wealth. Rather, one should oblige them to do all kinds of lowly work, such as keeping the streets clean or sweeping chimneys or, similarly, sweeping latrines and collecting dog droppings, etc.[42] And, in the meantime, one must not, as I have sometimes said, leave them the false book of the Talmud, but take it from them, and leave them nothing except the text of the Bible.[43] If that is done, I doubt not that they will adopt a different attitude and mode of thought. Then they would confess [the Christian faith] and leave their false beliefs behind and follow the truth of our faith.

Now I meekly beg of all those who have read this booklet or had it read to them not to get angry[44] at my words and deeds, for I did not mean [to involve] the innocent or expose them without cause or hand them over to the Christian authorities. I ask that I be kindly corrected, as should be done with anyone. Thus I submit myself at all times obediently to the Christian church. Amen.

This booklet was made and put together by me, Johannes Pfefferkorn, once a Jew, now a Christian, in the fifth year of my rebirth.[45] Issued[46] in Cologne on the Rhine, on the third day of January, [1]509. Printed in Augsburg.

**Notes**

1 See Kirn, *Das Bild,* 111 n. 267: 'Die mundartlich gefärbte Umschrift bestimmt den nach dürftigen Kenntnissen punktuierten, fehlerhaften Text' (The transliteration, tinged with dialect, is characteristic of the flawed text, the pointing of which betrays a poor knowledge).

2 The Latin version has 'Jewish animals' for 'Jews.'

3 The Latin version of this sentence is longer, expressing the hope that Christians will 'hear what serpents they nurse in their bosom (for Jews and Judaizers are the common enemies of all Christians), take precautions, and resist their fraud.'

4 The following examples also appear in a number of medieval polemics against Jews, for example, in the *Fortalitium fidei* (Fortress of Faith), composed by Alfonso de Spina in 1459 and printed in Strassburg c. 1471.

5 The two words mean 'Jesus of Nazareth.' Pfefferkorn's version 'seducer of the people' is an interpretation, not a translation. Here and elsewhere the sequence of the words printed in Hebrew is reversed, i.e., they must be read from left to right. This was corrected in the Latin version.

6 The printer has reversed the last two letters in 'Tholin' and turned the last letter upside down. The transliteration should be 'Tholui.' 'Hung' is a reference to Jesus' crucifixion.

7 There are repeated references in the Talmud to Jesus being a ממזר (bastard). Pfefferkorn's translation is discreet. Nevertheless he anticipated complaints that he was not discreet enough. See below, p. 62.

8 The Hebrew word means 'a woman who has been hung'; Pfefferkorn's translation is wrong.

9 Here, too, Pfefferkorn's translation is discreet. The Hebrew word means 'whore.'

10 In the transliteration, the word *yom* (day) is omitted. This is the only phrase in which the sequence of the words printed in Hebrew is correct.

11 The Latin version clarifies: 'the Eucharist, the true and living body of Christ.'

12 A reference to the tonsure of priests.

13 מוֹשָׁב can mean 'seat' or 'dwelling'; בֵּית כִּסֵּא means latrine. For the word order see above, n. 5.

14 The form is odd; the root of the word has two meanings, 'extermination' and 'conversion' or 'apostasy.'

15 The Latin version adds 'with their cursed eyes.'

16 Pfefferkorn provides the Hebrew and a transliteration in addition to the translation given here. The quotation comes from the 'Eighteen Benedictions' (*Shmoneh Esreh*) or 'Amidah' which are meant to be recited three times daily. The prayer is directed against apostates in general (including, but not exclusively referring to those who converted to Christianity). Pfefferkorn does not provide a translation for the last two lines quoted by him. They run: 'And may you speedily uproot, break, and defeat the kingdom of evil and cause the surrender of all our enemies, speedily in our days.' See also the following note.

17 Here Pfefferkorn paraphrases the last two lines of the prayer, interpreting the 'kingdom of evil' as a reference to the German Empire in his own day.

18 The Latin version adds: 'a superstition described in another volume.' The reference is to the booklet *Jewish Confession* (see Document 2, below).

19 The Hebrew and an interlinear transliteration follow. Pfefferkorn cites four lines (6, 7, 8, and 10 of 44 lines) from the prayer 'Avinu Malkeinu,' which is said during the concluding service of Yom Kippur.

20 Pfefferkorn provides a paraphrase that is partly wrong. The four lines mean: Destroy the plans of those who hate us; destroy the counsel of our enemies, destroy all of our enemies and adversaries; end pestilence, sword, hunger, captivity, destruction, and plague for the children of your covenant.

21 Pfefferkorn suggests that German 'seind' ('be' in the phrase 'be welcome') sounds like the Hebrew word for devil or demon, but his transliteration is wrong. See Reuchlin's argument below, Document 3.

22 The Latin version adds: 'because they consider us unclean and dirty, whereas they themselves are most unclean.'

23 The story is also told by Antonius Margarita, E iii verso.

24 A Gulden was the equivalent of 576 Heller, the currency used in Cologne, Pfefferkorn's place of residence. The pawnbroker in the example charged

interest at eight Hellers per week on one Gulden. This amounted to an annual interest of over seventy per cent.

25 Here follows a table showing the annual increase in principal and interest over a period of thirty years. Such tables were not new. They were printed repeatedly in the second half of the 15th century, as posters (broadsheets) and illustrations, for example, as the title page of Hans Folz, *Die Rechnung Ruprecht Kolpergers vor dem Gesuch der Juden* (The calculation of Ruprecht Kolperger in response to the application of the Jews), Nürnberg, 1480 (illustration 1, p. 68).

26 The Latin version clarifies: 'on their assertion, without regard for the law dictating that stolen goods be forfeited and publicly sold.' The privilege was abolished in 1548.

27 The Latin version clarifies: 'even if he bought them bona fide or accepted them under another just title.'

28 The Latin version elaborates: 'Listen to another crime by which the most criminal Jews grow rich. I will speak out openly that everyone may take precautions against their false pretenses and will not trust any of their statements regarding their income, and in the matter of contracts. Their usurious lending practices are an abuse and undue licence. When they have in their possession such letters and papers (since they have only fraudulent machinations on their mind), they reduce the figures and corrupt them and fraudulently imitate seals and counterfeit them, add other people's signatures, take some away or change them as they please and make new bills that have never been given into their hands and use the most fraudulent means that no counterfeiter has ever invented before. This is a frequent experience, and for this reason the most illustrious prince, the Emperor Maximilian, whom I mention with due honour, has expelled the Jews from many places in his realm, in Austria, Steiermark, and Kärnten, and decreed capital punishment for those convicted of fraud, although the culprit should have, by rights and by law, paid with his life and goods.'

29 The formula to be used by Jews was specified by the local authorities. Interestingly, it often included a reference to Jewish messianic hopes, for example in the Nürnberg formula of 1478: 'May neither my soul nor my body partake of the pledges given by God, and may my progeny never partake of the Messiah or the promised holy, blessed lands' (quoted by Kirn, *Das Bild*, 109 n. 256).

30 This paragraph appears only in the Latin version. It echoes the restrictions placed on Jews by the University of Paris: 'No Jew or Jewess may presume to operate surgically or medicinally on any person of Catholic faith. Also, since certain practitioners make or possess some medicines but totally

ignore their cause and reason, nay do not even know how to administer them and the relation which medicines have to disease, especially in all particular respects ... [they proceed] in certain cases rashly and to public scandal' (L. Thorndike, *University Records and Life in the Middle Ages* [New York, 1944], 83–4).

31 Jews were in fact renowned for their medical knowledge and throughout history have significantly contributed to the progress of medical science. The practice of medicine was one of the few respected professions open to Jews in Europe at the time. 'Rabbi Moses and Isaac' may be a reference to the famous Jewish philosophers and physicians Moses Maimonides (1135–1204) and Meir b. Isaac Aldabi (c. 1310–c. 1360).

32 The Latin version adds: 'or appeal the case or tire the Christian out with expenses, so that he is forced to desist, or effect that the Jew is completely acquitted or wins, if he is the one who brought the action. The Christian is defeated, naturally, because the Jew is richer than the Christian and can spend more money. I name no names, nor is this my task. Thus no one can rightly be angry with me, unless he confesses that it concerns him. It is clear that this is so.'

33 The Latin version is gender neutral: 'Christian men and women (to give each his or her due).'

34 The Latin version explains 'allies' as 'men hired by them and paid to do the deed, which they strive for and attempt, but I do not show myself among them.'

35 Pefferkorn quotes two passages from the Old Testament (Zach 9:9 and Dan 9:26) that are interpreted by Christians as references to Jesus.

36 The temple was destroyed by the Romans in 70 AD.

37 Pfefferkorn quotes Is. 1:11–15 and Jer. 31:31–2, which are used by Christian interpreters to disparage sacrifices.

38 The Latin version adds: 'and like a tavern or inn.'

39 The Latin version adds: 'Some may perhaps think that it was not at all necessary that Johannes Pfefferkorn, in writing against the Jews and bringing this to people's notice, make use of the novelty of inserting Hebrew writing and words. For we have Latin doctors of Holy Writ and books with which to confront the Jews when we dispute with them. Yet they cannot be drawn away from their error or are unwilling to abandon it, although they are plainly refuted in the books that we have received from them through translators. When they say so, I reply, with due respect: If a Christian is ever so learned, when he disputes with a Jew on the basis of the Bible and after he has defeated the Jew with arguments taken from the words and meaning of the Bible, and the defeated man cannot rebut him, he uses fallacies and fraudulent reasons. He says to

the Christian: 'You cite many scriptural passages that sound different in my Hebrew Bible and are interpreted in a different way;' and with such words they look down on and disdain the Latin books. They are called among them in Hebrew "sforim pselim," that is, abandoned or rejected books, or disapproved books. Moved by such reasoning, I put Hebrew words taken from their sources, convincing them on the basis of their own words and deeds that the books of Moses and the words of the prophets are deceitful, and I use the testimony of Christian truth against their perfidy, showing the underlying agreement with the Latin Bible and showing that there is no discrepancy in the words, not to speak of their meaning, as I have shown above. Thus no Jew will ever be able to argue against them.'

40 The Latin version adds: 'and that it may be read in Latin as well by those who know this language, I engaged the help of some people to translate it from German into Latin.'

41 The Latin version has 'Jewish animals' for 'them.'

42 The Latin version adds: 'take away the cadavers of animals and skin them and such duties.'

43 The Latin version elaborates: 'no text that concerns and relates to religion, faith, laws, and sacred rites, except the Bible, and to search their libraries at home and in the synagogues and interrogate them even under torture, lest they conceal them.'

44 The Latin version adds: 'I know the iniquity of the Jews and have exposed it that it might be avoided, punished, and prohibited. I exhort the Christian rulers to enforce this. In this matter, if I seem to speak rather freely and with greater licence than I ought to do and is my place, thereby offending my betters and the rulers of the Christian church ...'

45 That is, his baptism in 1504.

46 The Latin version reads: Issued in Cologne, printed by me, Heinrich of Hussia, on the 9th of March, in the year of the Lord 1509.

# Die rechnūg Ruprecht Kolpergers vō dē gesuch der iuden auf 30 dn̄

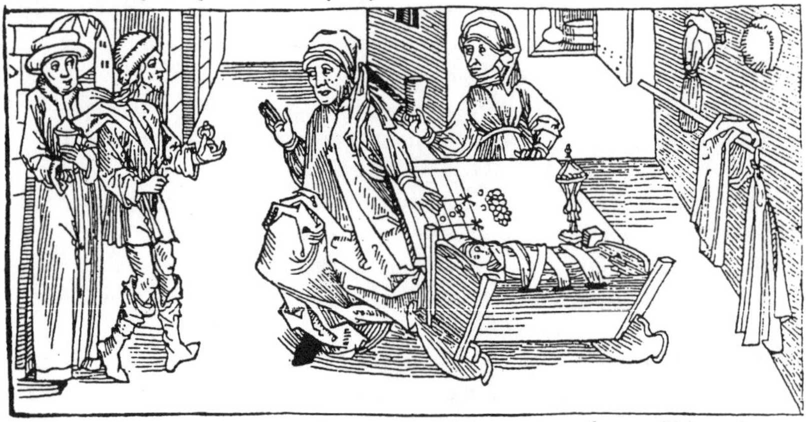

| | | |
|---|---|---|
| 1 Jar | 61 | dn̄ |
| 2 Jar | 124 | dn̄ |
| 3 Jar | 254 | dn̄ |
| 4 Jar | 523 | dn̄ |
| 5 Jar | 1082 | dn̄ |
| 6 Jar | 2241 | dn̄ |
| 7 Jar | 4645 | dn̄ |
| 8 Jar | 9630 | dn̄ |
| 9 Jar | 19908 | dn̄ |
| 10 Jar | 41403 | dn̄ |
| 11 Jar | 85840 | dn̄ |
| 12 Jar | 178017 | dn̄ |
| 13 Jar | 369134 | dn̄ |
| 14 Jar | 765434 | dn̄ |
| 15 Jar | 1587201 | dn̄ |
| 16 Jar | 3291218 | dn̄ |
| 17 Jar | 6824667 | dn̄ |
| 18 Jar | 14151628 | dn̄ |
| 19 Jar | 29344813 | dn̄ |
| 20 Jar | 60849403 | dn̄ |
| Suma | 243397 fl 5 lb 3 dn̄ | |

Etwas zu sagē von den iudē
vn̄ den v̄fluchtē teifels iuden
so merckt wie wol ir eim ei kint
gepoern wirt ist er drauf besint
das er im xxx pfenig lahen dut
doch anders nit dan in dem mut
vnd eigentlich der meinung nach
das es aln cristen sei ein schmach
dar vm das vnser schöpfer zart
vm xxx pfening verkauffet wart
des halb er mer noch minder nimpt
dar auff vns dan hin wider zimpt
zu sagen das xxx iuden plut
vm einen pfenig verkauffet sint
des halb ich plint sie nenen mag
wan sie nie hant erkant den tag
dar in sie got do selbst det straffen
vnd hant die bitten pfaff v̄schlaffē
irs messias halben die narn
dar auff sie ye seit laurn vnd harn
Nun das bestee nach seiner war
die xxx pfening leicht er ym dar
all virteil iars vm sechs gesuch
vnd im zu eim ewigen fluch
wan yn das zehend pot dut lern
du solt nit fremdes guts begern
Nun slecht er vier mol vm ym iar
als sie über al thū für war
vnd ist geflissen tag vnd nacht
gar zu verderben cristlich macht
praucht doch dar pei des fortals sich
er sagt dem cristē wie frauntlich
ym in der rechnung sol geschen
er well yn gar vil übersehen
lest im gleich wol nit wenig nach
das man destminnd merck sein rach
war aber es die xx iar raichet
stet in den ziffern klar verzaichet
vnd nimāt glaupt d sum auff erdē
des halb es offenbar muß werden
So aber nū nit ider man
sich noch den ziffern richten kan
hab ich das auch von iar zu iar
zu reym gesagt gantz offenbar
Das erst iar ein vn̄ sechtzg .dn̄.macht
das ander hundert xxiiii sacht
das drit ccl vnd fir
funffhundert xxiii mir
das fird nach woren rechnūg stipt
dē funfften .m. zwei vn̄achtzig zipt
so macht das .vi. nach rechtē schrit
zwei .m. zwei c ein vnd firtzick
Fier .m. vnd vi hundert wist
vn̄ funf vnd xxx pringend ist
das sibēd iar Das acht merck fleisig
naiu .m.sechs.c.vnd dreissig
das neünd neünzehen tausent hot
nein.c.acht vnd sechtzg von not
Daß.x.ein vnd virtzig tausent
do fier hundert vnd dreú pei hausen
Fünf vn̄ achtzig tausent acht hūdt
vn̄.l.das eylft iar macht mit wūdt
hūdt tausent das .xii.iar inist
mit acht vn̄ sibentzg tausent wist
vnd sibentzehen auch dar pei
Merckt was das.xiii. iar aus schrei
wol drei mol hūdt tausent ich
mit naün vn̄ sechtzg tausentē sprich
dar pei hūdert vn̄ fier vnd dreissig
sint auch dar zu besumet fleisig
Das fiertzhent iar zu siben moln
hundert tausent pfenig dut holn
mit fünf vnd sechzig tausent der
fierhundert fier vnd dreissig sint mer
Das fünfzend iar ist dar bestimpt
den zu tausent moln tausent zimpt
vnd fünf mol hūdtausent me

1 Table of annual increase in principal and interest

DOCUMENT 2

# Johann Pfefferkorn

## *The Confession of the Jews*

The following translation is based on the German text printed by Jörg Nadler, Augsburg 1508 (Ai recto–Cii recto). It appeared in Latin from the press of Johannes Landen, Nürnberg, 1508. Important variants are pointed out in the notes. The book deserves special attention for the illustrations it contains. As noted by Richard Cohen, who examined the iconography in books printed in early modern Europe, the illustrations signal a new phase in the depiction of Jews.[1] Although the accompanying text remains hostile toward the Jews, the illustrations move away from the customary emphasis on Jewish 'perfidy' and offer instead authentic representations of Jewish customs. The illustration on the title page shows the inside of a synagogue, where Rosh Hashanah is celebrated with the blowing of the ram's horn. There are other realistic details: The ark with the curtain pulled to one side; the cantor at the lectern; women and children segregated from the men. A second illustration shows the Tashlikh ceremony, a ritual casting of sins to the wind and to the fish in a stream; the third represents the Kapparot ceremony, another purification rite, in which the believers transfer their sins to a rooster. The final illustration shows the Yom Kippur service with the priestly benediction and a ritual flogging. The only remnant of the traditional iconography is the shroud-covered eyes of the Jewish worshippers, which signal their moral and spiritual 'blindness.' The illustrations proved popular and were reprinted in Antonius Margarita's *Der gantz jüdisch Glaub* (The Whole Jewish Faith) a generation later.

## *The Confession of the Jews*

I am a booklet entitled *Confession of the Jews*, readily encountered everywhere, full of new knowledge. I wish to be distributed widely in all countries. I wish my readers well but do not want to be shared with Jews.[2]

### *The Preface*

In honour and praise of our beloved Lord Jesus Christ, of his blessed mother Mary, Heavenly Queen, Immaculate Virgin forever, and of the heavenly host I have taken on the task of publishing and revealing the rite of confession practised by the blind Jews: how they prepare themselves, how and to whom they confess, and who absolves them from their sins. Thus every prudent person may take note of these rites, which have no foundation, and may reject them and be in a better position to show them the right way. Unfortunately I myself was for a long time under these delusions, but now through God's mercy I have abandoned them and have entered into the light of the Christian faith. May I continue in this course and keep to it with God's help, for we ourselves are powerless on our own and can rely only on the gift and mercy of God. Therefore I beg all Christians to pray on behalf of this poor sinner to the eternal God in heaven that he may be gracious and merciful and forgive my sins and give me the strength and understanding to battle against the cruel enemy of Christ and of his dear mother Mary; and that I may always be obedient to the teaching and instruction of my betters who are learned in the Christian faith, as is fair and righteous. Amen.

Item, I wish to divide this booklet into six parts. The first part concerns the preparations for the Jewish confession; the second, how they confess and who absolves them; the third, why I have revealed and proffered this matter; the fourth, what great damage and dishonour arises and comes to those who associate and socialize too much with Jews; the fifth contains a respectful admonition to the Christian princes, who accommodate and protect the Jews; the sixth explains the reason why many Jews, who in their hearts are inclined to believe in Jesus, retain nevertheless their Jewish way of life. Thus I want to begin in the name of God with the first part.

Of the preparation of Jews for the confession, at what time this takes place and in what manner

*Chapter 1*

The time when Jews wish (and are customarily obliged) to make their confession and lament their sins begins on the 1st of the month of August. They prepare for it with great devotion, proceeding in this manner: They rise early in the morning, two hours before sunrise, and go to their synagogue and pray for an hour or two during the day. And they return to the synagogue in the evening. At that time a ram's horn is sounded, which calls them to the repentance of their sins and to reconciliation with God, just as we Christians are admonished by the preacher during Lent. For their admonition the ram's horn is blown morning and evening throughout the aforesaid month, and the devotions are maintained, as I said. They pray that God will forgive their sins, deliver them from their enemies, lead them back into the city of Jerusalem, and stand by them in the building of the temple of Solomon, so that they may sacrifice cows, calves, and sheep and other things, according to the tradition of their fathers and forefathers. On the last day of the aforesaid month, which they consider New Year's Eve,[3] young and old, men and women, prepare to bathe and wash and purify their entire body. After the ablutions they all wade into a river and submerge themselves completely three times, crying out and saying: 'Alas, I too am one of the sinful human beings.' They believe that they are purified once they have cleansed their bodies in this manner. They do this on the basis of chapter 23 of the Book Leviticus.[4] The next day, that is, the first day of the month of September, which is their New Year's Day and a great feast and holiday, they rise early at dawn and go to their synagogues, according to the 22nd chapter of Genesis, where it is written that Abraham rose early in the morning in obedience to the command of his Lord and God, for God had commanded him to sacrifice his son Isaac.[5] They believe that they are following the example of Abraham by rising early and, like him, offer an acceptable sacrifice to God. They cover their heads with a white linen cloth with fringes at the four corners which they take into their hands, contemplate, and stroke themselves with, while they contemplate the commandments of God, which Moses, instructed by God, bid them to observe. When they are assembled thus in their synagogue, divided in such a manner that married and unmarried women are in a place separate from the men, the wealthiest and most respected man in the synagogue rises and goes to the ark, in which the five books of Moses are kept, and begins to speak as the representative and emissary of the people. He praises the Lord our God and gives thanks on behalf of the whole people for God having sanctified them with this command to cleanse their hands and for having given roosters the intelligence to distinguish between night and day. And he thanks God on behalf of the men for not having made them women or Christians or slaves of another nation.[6]

Oh, how blind and ignorant is this poor and wretched people! It is obvious that in the whole world there is nothing more wretched and distressing than they. They have been driven and dispersed over the whole wide world, abandoned by God to perpetual misery, from which they may never be delivered except through the Christian faith!

Next, the said representative who stands before the ark of God, begs God to protect them from evil people, evil thoughts and bad company, bad neighbours, and the uncircumcised (that is, us Christians) and from the devil and severe judgment. Next they recall the sacrifice offered by their forefathers of lambs, cows, sheep, and rams, and how their priests in former times diligently offered cakes of wheat, honey, and oil. Everything is done in great piety and devotion. The psalter is read in great awe by the said representative, according to the plain text, with certain gestures, as they also do with other passages. For example, when they read in the prophet Isaiah 'Holy, holy, holy is God,' they jump up very energetically. For they interpret the commandment of Moses literally, when he commanded them to love the Lord with all the strength of their body. They then remind God of the pledge and promise to Abraham, as is written in Genesis 22 [:17], when he said: ' I shall bless your seed above all nations of the world, that it may multiply and be in number like the stars of heaven and the sands of the sea,' and they pray to God that he may send them the Messiah to deliver them and lead them to salvation.

As the aforesaid representative standing before the ark beseeches and prays to God, the others do likewise and join him in long prayers taken from the great books they have in front of them. But their prayers lack reason and understanding. Thereafter they deliberate how they may obtain power and domination over the world, how they may obtain secular goods, and avenge themselves on us Christians – they have no other thought. They call for and beg for the Messiah, who has already been sent, God and man, born of their own race. Thus their hopes are in vain, as were the long-standing hopes of their forefathers whom they imitate. The said prayers last from three until about eight o'clock in the morning.

Next, the five books of Moses, beautifully inscribed on good clean parchment and rolled up, are taken out of the ark and are placed on the altar.[7] Several chapters from it are read. Then one, who has been chosen and appointed to this task, takes the scroll with both hands and lifts it above his head, so that everyone may see it, and carries it around three times in a circle, while the congregation calls out in clear, loud voices: 'This is the commandment, which Moses gave a long time ago to our forefathers, the children of Israel, and which he commanded us to observe.' Then the parchment is rolled up again, and the Rabbi sitting by the altar, holds the heavy scroll resting on his right arm. Next, the person who is in charge of blowing the horn, as I explained earlier on, comes up and stands devoutly beside the altar, and the people remain in deep devotion, repenting of their sins.

The rabbi, who sits by the altar with the scroll, says: 'Blow your horn.'[8] And so it is done. He blows into the horn ten times, as bidden by the rabbi. Then the rabbi tells him: 'Cease for a while blowing your horn.' Shortly afterwards he asks him again to blow the horn ten times, then to rest again. This is done three times, and everyone faithfully believes that his sins are taken away through the sound of the horn. If the sound of the horn is clear and sharp and not harsh and dull, they are most joyful and believe that a good and fortunate year lies ahead; but if the horn does not sound right, and is rather harsh, they are grieved and say: 'Alas, the coming year will be bad and bring persecution from the Christians.' Then the books of Moses are once again locked up in the ark, at which they all begin to cry in disorderly fashion and say: 'O father and king, we have sinned before your face, the will of your divine name be done, drive out and deliver us from all evil temptations and evil thoughts and avenge our enemies and destroy all who wish us evil and have in mind to do us injury. Destroy them with pestilence and all plagues, for the sake of your circumcised children, whom you have chosen, etc.'[9]

And if they want to deny that this is so, one may obtain proof of it out of their own books, in which these prayers are found. This execration applies specifically to us Christians, and to no one else. Thus my loyal advice, according to my modest understanding, is to take from them the books containing these execrations and not leave them in their possesssion, even if their malicious prayer and desire can do us no harm, as the Prophet Isaiah says in the first chapter: 'They shall not be heard.'[10] Nevertheless, speaking in human terms, this must not be suffered. It would, moreover, benefit the Jews not to have these books any more. Thus their evil customs would gradually fall into oblivion.

The rites I have described continue until twelve o'clock noon. Let this be the end of the chapter describing how the Jews prepare for confession.

*Chapter 2*

At twelve o'clock noon they leave the synagogue and go to a clear flowing river to bathe.[11] They turn to face downstream and, gathering their clothes up in front, they shake them out, and call out from the bottom of their hearts to the fish: 'We are casting our sins to you. Receive them.' They are convinced that the fish will take it upon themselves to eat their foul sins. If it so happens, however, that the Jews live in an area where there is no running water nearby which they might reach, they wait and pray for a great storm, turn their faces away from the wind and, while shaking out their clothes into the wind, say the same words that they say to the fish, as earlier mentioned. Now someone might ask why they do not turn their faces into the wind. They act in this manner thinking that the sins will be carried away from them by the water and wind and to avoid their being carried back to them. They have adopted this strange method without any basis or reason. It is neither written nor commanded nor prefigured by examples in the Old Testament. Rather it has been instituted and arranged in the Talmud and by their other false rabbis, whom they obey and in whom they believe more firmly than in Holy Scripture.[12] These rabbis interpret it according to their own will, not according to the meaning of Moses and the prophets, as handed down in scripture. This confession is called by the Jews 'the minor confession' and takes place on the first day of the autumn month.

After the aforesaid confession they do great penance for nine days in a row, fasting to discipline and castigate their body, each according to his ability and interpretation. Every day they visit the synagogue, and on the ninth day of penitence, after returning from the temple to their house, every man, young and old, takes a white rooster and every female, married or unmarried, a white hen for themselves and for the unborn who has not yet committed a sin but was conceived in carnal desire.[13] Each one holds his rooster or hen, with the head of the household standing in the midst of his family, silent and in deep devotion, contemplating for some time their sins, And when he has contemplated them, he takes his rooster by the legs and swings him around his head three times, so that the rooster flutters his wings and strikes the man. Then he says to the rooster: 'You deliver me from my sins, which have been turned over and transferred to you. I am now free of my sins. You, however, have taken over my guilt. You meet death, I go on to eternal life.' Then each one takes his rooster and acts like the head of the household, imitating his gestures and ritual, with great sorrow for their sins and devoutly asking for God's mercy. And they are firmly convinced and believe that their sins are now completely pardoned and forgiven. Then they take the roosters and hens, suffocate them, and fry or boil them. They then prepare to bathe and diligently rub and wash their entire body, in case any sin remains or is concealed or was forgotten, thinking that it has now been washed off.

Thereafter they again go to a river, dive in once so that their whole body is out of sight, then wade ashore and don a white linen dress and prepare to eat. If someone thinks, however, that he is not completely cleansed and has feelings of bad conscience, he goes to his nearest friends or neighbours in the synagogue, kneels down, and bends his head down to the floor. The other man lifts up the sinner's clothes at the back and strikes him with a leather belt or in some other fashion strikes his behind thirty-nine times.[14] Thus any remaining sin escapes through his behind, and the man is completely clean and pure.

As evening approaches they joyfully sit down at table and eat their confessors and their own sins until they are sated. After the dinner they don a dress of cotton and linen made for this occasion, and each person lights a beautiful candle, which he keeps burning that evening and the following day, which is called the Day of Atonement. A Christian is present to prevent any harm. They themselves do not touch the candle to avoid interrupting the celebration.[15] But if a steer or a cow or another useful animal falls into a cellar or ditch, the whole congregation would soon come running to its aid, without a thought about breaking off the celebration.

On the said day, after the meal, the rabbis usually go and eat in the synagogue and remain there for a part of the night alone. At three o'clock in the morning, [that is,] after midnight, everyone goes to the synagogue, except the unmarried young women, who remain at home. Women and men walk separately, barefoot with their shoes off. They set out and begin their new year by calling on God and praying that God may lead them to the city of Jerusalem and build the temple, etc., and many other fruitless prayers. They have one prayer in particular, in which they say that other nations (they mean us Christians) practise idolatry and call on a God who cannot help anyone, and they boast that they pray to the king who is King of Kings. In this prayer the name 'king' is said three times, denoting the Holy Trinity, which they do not wish to understand in their hardened malice and recalcitrance. Next they shout and call in a clear voice, saying: 'You are our God, and no other.' By this they mean to indicate that Christ, the son of Mary, who has delivered us from the power of the devil and from eternal damnation through his precious blood on the sacred wooden cross, is no God. This prayer of theirs is called in Hebrew 'olenni laschabeha,' [It is our duty to pray] and is a daily prayer.[16]

When all these things have been done, everyone, young and old, gathers, who is born from the tribe of Aaron, who were once priests but are no longer priests now. They stand before the ark with great piety and devotion, raise their hands up high, as you can see in this illustration, that is, they bless the people, after the direction in the Book of Numbers, chapter 6 [:25–6], saying: 'May God shine the light of his face on you, that you may rest in his grace. May God turn his face toward you and bring you joy.' This prayer and blessing is repeated three times on that day, and while those from the tribe of Aaron raise up their hands to bless the people, no one of the Jews, nor they themselves, must look at their hands for this reason: They are completely convinced and do not doubt that the spirit of the Lord is resting on their hands and believe that anyone who willingly looks at them will die at this very hour. They take this out of the 28th chapter of the Book Exodus ...[17]

Why I know this and have brought this custom into the light of day and how one may deliver some Jews from their malice

*Chapter 3*

First I have revealed the bad custom of the Jews, which has no foundation, so that anyone may understand my view in this matter. This is my purpose: that they may be mocked and reproved for this custom and perhaps abandon their errors on account of the ridicule, and be moved to turn to the light of the Christian faith. Now, one may say, they have been reproved and yet they remain blind and keep to their purpose. To this I reply: that may be so, I admit it, but according to my lights I shall use a comparison and thereby touch on two good reasons why sins become ingrained and increase. Unfortunately one encounters many Christians who lead a reprehensible and disorderly and ungodly life, one through usury, another through fraudulent commerce, and many other sins which I need not enumerate. Such an indecent disorderly life mostly derives from two sources: first, they have seen such behaviour from childhood on in their parents and think and believe that it is well done. Thus they follow in their footsteps. The other reason is this: they have practised it and lived this life for such a long time that bad habits have blinded and hardened them and they have lost their sense of decency and no longer regard it as a sin, great or small. When such people come to hear a sermon in which this kind of life is placed clearly before their eyes, an inner spark of understanding in their hearts moves them to reflect on their actions which are against Christian law and to consider that they will not achieve eternal bliss in this manner. On account of such thoughts they sometimes stop their wicked life and improve, but their change of heart comes from and originates in the sermon; and if they had not heard the admonition, they would not have thought about it. And this is also the case with the Jews. They are rooted in their bad habits through the example of their parents, and following their example, they think that their actions are good rather than bad, but if they came to hear a sermon, even if they were forced to listen to a sermon in which their condemned life is held up to them clearly and ridiculed, a spark of understanding would enter their hearts too and they would say to themselves: Observe that the law of nature is ordained rightly and correctly. Do not do to another what you do not wish to happen to yourself. Why do you curse Christians every day, when you yourself would not like it if it happened to you? Furthermore they would think and say in their heart: Look at the five books of Moses and the prophets and all of sacred scripture, look at your own life and that of your rabbis, all of whom have lied to us about our Messiah, speaking of a future time at which we shall be saved, whereas it has long since come to pass. Oh, we have been miserably deceived. Where are our prophets? None of them has been with us for a long time. And although such thoughts and reflections would not completely make them abandon their errors, they would do so gradually, day by day, and in due course approach the path to bliss. Furthermore it would be a useful, right, and godly action to take from them the Talmud and other false rabbinical books, together with their prayer books that contain bad precepts and customs, and to completely destroy them. Without a doubt they would then in time forget their bad habits, as I said before. I place my firm hope and trust in the Almighty God, that through such intentions and attempts they would shortly come out of their darkness onto the path of eternal light and knowledge of the Christian faith ...

An admonition to Christian princes and other estates who house, shelter, and protect Jews

*Chapter 5*

With your permission I will say something else in a submissive and modest spirit. You Christian princes, cities, and others house, shelter, defend, and protect Jews, who are sacrilegious and merciless enemies of our God and of the holy Christian faith, in your cities and other places for the sake of a small fleeting, inane, and sinful profit. In consequence, these execrable and cursed bloodhounds suck your poor wretched subjects' blood and take away what they have sweated for. This must necessarily happen, for they cannot support themselves in any other way than through usury. Ponder and consider well in your innermost hearts: when they give or hand over to you one Gulden, they take in return hundreds of Gulden, impoverishing your poor subjects or taking interest from them[18] or whatever you want to call it. Thus the country and people, cities and other places suffer the most wretched harm and damage. May God have mercy on them. Furthermore, if you are faithful stewards of the holy Christian church, consider the shameful and evil deeds of the Jews, who curse and desecrate the almighty God, Mary who has given us Jesus Christ, and all the heavenly host and the whole of Christendom, and commit other evil deeds. In justice and loyalty to Christianity, you should not let them go scot free and go empty-handed yourselves. Drive them out of your lands or forbid them to charge interest. Let them work as we Christians must work and force them to hear the word of God, whether they are willing or not, as I said earlier, lest on the day of the Last Judgment you fall short in giving your account of this matter to almighty God. Merciful God, alas, I know that there are many towns and cities where the Jews are more respected than Christians and preferred to them. The princes say their forefathers have admitted them, and call the Jews the loyal treasurers of the common man and say that in case of a true emergency, their goods and possessions would be handed over and put to common use. Here, too, they put up with and protect the execrable Jews, saying that they have a great privilege from emperors and kings, guaranteeing their liberties, and if they violated this privilege, the outcome and result would be disgrace and tumult and harm. That is what they say to the common people. Oh, those who speak thus, using pretence and concealment, blind and stop up the eyes of justice and prudence by embellishing sins! I fear that those who suffer and permit the Jews to burden poor Christians and impoverish them and militate against and deride God, bear no less responsibility than did Pilate who was guilty of the death of Christ, even though he washed his hands of it to appear innocent before the people. For we find written that the person who confesses his guilt or allows sinful deeds to happen when he might fight them or prevent them is just as guilty and subject to punishment as if he had committed the sin himself. Were there not once Jews in many towns, cities, and lands, for example, in France, Spain, Denmark, and until recently in Nürnberg, Ulm, Nördlingen, etc.? And have they not been driven out?[19] I am asking: what harm or ill will result from their expulsion? If the authorities have done well and acted in fairness, you should imitate them for the salvation of your soul.

I want to end here and conclude my booklet and peacefully and modestly ask all who read it or have it read to them kindly to correct anything that is badly put or may be harmful; and, as far as each one is able, to see to it that the poor blinded Jews are brought to the recognition of the Christian faith and are held to it and instructed in it. For this they will undoubtedly receive no small reward here and in future from our Lord God, to whom we give praise and glory for ever and ever. Amen.

This booklet has been made and put together by Johannes Pfeff[e]rkorn, formerly a Jew, now a Christian, and was then printed in Augsburg by Jörg Nadler in 1508.

**Notes**

1 See illustrations 2–5, pp. 82–5. For a discussion of the illustrations, see R. Cohen, *Jewish Icons: Art and Society in Modern Europe* (Berkeley, 1998), 16–22.

2 The Latin edition of the work, entitled *Libellus de Judaica confessione* (A Booklet about the Jewish Confession) contains a more hostile prefatory poem: 'If you wish to know who I am, I shall tell you: a booklet, brief and easy, about the sacred time of purification for Jews, the day on which they rid themselves of their sins and by what rites of purification. I make public the vain fantasies of the Jewish people, which cannot obtain for

itself hope of salvation. Oh, condemn them – thus God the judge of what is right will save you.'

3 I.e., Rosh Hashana. The descriptions of the ceremonies are accurate unless otherwise noted.

4 Lev. 23:24–5 states: 'The seventh month, on the first day of the month, you shall keep a sabbath, a memorial, with the sound of trumpets, and it shall be called holy. You shall do no servile work therein, and you shall offer a holocaust to the Lord.'

5 Gen. 22:13. The ram's horn (shofar) commemorates God's mercy. He spared Issac and permitted Abraham to substitute a ram for his son.

6 This is a paraphrase of the Birkhot ha-shachar prayer, originally a morning benediction.

7 The ark is a built-in cupboard in the east wall of the synagogue. It is curtained and contains the scrolls of the Torah (the first five books of the Old Testament, known to Christians as the Pentateuch).

8 As described in the following passage, the ram's horn is blown after the reading from the 'five books of Moses' (i.e., the Torah; see preceeding note). Three different notes are sounded three times, followed by a fourth long, drawn-out tone. This ceremony is repeated three times.

9 This prayer (Avinu malkenu = Our father, our king) was recited on fast days. It is mentioned in the Talmud (Ta'an 25 b).

10 Is 1:15.

11 The following paragraph describes the Tashlikh ceremony.

12 Contrary to Pfefferkorn's claims, the rite is not mentioned in the Talmud and is based on scripture, i.e., Micah 7:19, 'You will cast all their sins into the depths of the sea.' The ceremony takes its name from the scriptural passage (tashlikh = you will cast out).

13 The following paragraph describes the Kapparot ceremony. The Hebrew term means 'expiations.' The custom is not mentioned in the Talmud; it made its first appearance in the writings of the geonim during the ninth century.

14 The Torah specifies that punishment by flagellation must consist of 'less than forty' lashes. Richard Cohen, *Jewish Icons*, wrongly assumes that Pfefferkorn 'concocted' this ceremony (20). It is documented in sixteenth-century Germany and France. Cf. *The Oxford Dictionary of Jewish Religion* (1997), 751. Margaret Olin brought to my attention a review of Cohen's book in *The New Republic* (25 Sept. 2000), 48. The author, Elliott Horowitz, points out Cohen's mistake and attests to the continued practice in contemporary Israel: 'I myself have been offered (but declined) the privilege of being whipped, with something resembling a shoelace, while visiting the ritual bath in my Jerusalem neighborhood on Yom Kippur

eve. One of these years I hope to bring Professor Cohen along, so that he can atone for his error.'

15 The illustration shows a Christian relighting the candle. Significantly, he is the only figure whose eyes are not shrouded, i.e., who is not 'blind.' Orthodox Jews were afraid of breaking the biblical commandment dictating that no 'servile work' be done on the feast day: 'And every soul that shall do any work, the same will I destroy' (Lev. 23:30).

16 I.e., the Aleinu prayer, which came to be recited at the end of every service.

17 Ex. 28:41

18 Pfefferkorn uses the word 'schatzen,' which means to tax.

19 In France Jews were expelled from individual counties in the fifteenth century. After their expulsion from Provence in 1501, few Jewish communities remained. Spain expelled the Jews in 1492. They were driven out of Nürnberg in 1498, Ulm in 1499, and Nördlingen in 1507. Cf. M. Wenninger, *Man bedarf keiner Juden mehr: Ursachen und Hintergründe ihrer Vertreibung aus den deutschen Reichsstädten im 15. Jahrhundert* (Vienna, 1981).

2 A synagogue during the celebration of Rosh Hashanah

3 The Tashlikh ceremony

4 The Kapparot ceremony

5 The Yom Kippur service

**DOCUMENT 3**

# Johann Reuchlin

## *Report about the Books of the Jews*

Reuchlin's report, dated 6 October 1510, was addressed to Uriel, archbishop of Mainz, who chaired the imperial commission investigating Pfefferkorn's proposal to confiscate the books of the Jews. It was confidential, but Pfefferkorn apparently obtained access to it and referred to its contents in the *Hand Mirror*, published in the spring of 1511. In reply, Reuchlin issued the *Eye Mirror* (Tübingen, 1511),[1] which contained an annotated version of his report and a brief account of the circumstances that led to its publication. The account and the report are in German, as was the original sent to the archbishop. The annotations by contrast are in Latin, that is, aimed at a scholarly audience. It was this book rather than the original report that was condemned by the Cologne theologians and, ultimately, by the papal court in Rome.

The following translation is based on the text in *Johannes Reuchlin: Gutachten über das Jüdische Schrifttum*, ed. and trans. into modern German by Antonie Leinz-v. Dessauer (Stuttgart, 1965), 28–105. Reuchlin supports his opinion with detailed references to imperial and canon law. I have omitted these references.

### *Report about the Books of the Jews*

As an obedient subject I have received with due respect the commission of His Majesty, the most exalted and eminent prince and lord, Lord Maximilian, Roman emperor, our most noble master, given first to Your Princely Grace[2] and now conveyed and given to me.[3] In it I am commanded to examine with due diligence the matter of the books of the Jews concerning the laws of Moses, the prophets, and the Psalms of the Old Testament in their current version, which have been confiscated or designated as suspect, and to give an opinion on how and on what basis one ought to approach the whole matter and proceed with it, and especially, whether the destruction of such writings would glorify God and benefit the holy Christian faith and help promote piety.

Although I am conscious of being much too insignificant to answer such great questions of law that concern the welfare of the Christian church and the reputation and honour of the Roman Imperial Majesty, I will nevertheless in obedience to my duty prefer to be judged unwise by everyone rather than disobedient. Thus I shall write down my modest opinions on the question, as follows:

Whether the books of the Jews ought to be confiscated, destroyed, or burned, and if this can be done legally:

Some people answer in the affirmative, giving many reasons:

1 Because they are supposedly composed against Christians
2 Because they insult Jesus, Mary, and the twelve apostles, and also our Christian law
3 Because they are supposedly false
4 Because they motivate Jews to remain in their Jewish faith and keep them from turning to the Christian faith

Anyone who could prevent such great evil and does not prevent or put an end to it, must be regarded as being at equal fault as the doer, and should be punished as an abetter.

But there are also people who deny this, and not without giving reasons:

1 The Jews are subjects of the Holy Roman Empire and are to be treated according to imperial law.
2 Our property must not be taken away against our will.
3 Imperial and royal law, as well as the decrees of princes, say that no one should lose his possessions by force.
4 Everyone is entitled to his old customs, traditions, and possessions, even a robber.
5 Thus the Jews should keep their synagogues, which are called 'schul,' in peace, without harassment and interference.
6 None of the writings of the Jews has been rejected or condemned, either by secular or by ecclesiastical authorities.

It is for these reasons that these people think one should not take those books away from the Jews, suppress, or burn them.
In God's name. Amen.

To answer the question [whether action should be taken against the books of the Jews], one ought further to consider and distinguish between wheat and weed, so as not to pull up one with the other, as the holy gospel says (Matt. 13). Now, I find that the books of the Jews are of several kinds:

1 Holy Scripture, which they call 'Essrim Varba,' that is 'twenty-four,' for their Bible has twenty-four books
2 The Talmud, which is a collection of teachings and explanations of the precepts and prohibitions given to them in the Torah, that is, the five books of Moses, of which 613 [teachings] were written down a long time ago by their great scholars
3 The most secret speech and words of God, which they call 'Cabala'
4 Glosses and commentaries written by scholars and scribes on every book of the Bible. They call such comments or commentaries 'Perusch'[4]
5 Sermons, disputations, prayerbooks called 'Midrasch' or 'Draschoth'[5]
6 Books of philosophers and scholars of all disciplines; they are generally called 'Sepharim,' that is, books, and designated according to the scholar or discipline
7 Finally, there are poetry, fables, verse, tales, satires, and collections of didactic examples, each with their own title, as devised by the author. Most of these the Jews themselves regard as fiction and invention.

Among the last mentioned books some may be found perhaps (but only very few) which ridicule, slander, and insult our dear Lord and God Jesus and his Mother, and the apostles and saints. I have read only two such books: one called *Nizzachon*, the other *Tolduth Jeschu ha nozri*.[6] Even the Jews themselves regard them as apocryphal, as Paulus Burgensis writes in the second part of his *Scrutinium*, chapter 6.[7] Indeed when I was previously at the court of Frederick III, our gracious lord's father of blessed memory,[8] I heard the Jews themselves say in the frequent conversations I had with them that they have removed and destroyed such books and forbidden that people should in future write such books or speak thus.

Now, to proceed to the question at hand, I have this to say: If it is found that a Jew knowingly keeps such a book which has been expressly and clearly printed to insult and shame and dishonour our Lord God Jesus, his mother, the saints, or the Christian law, the book should be taken away and burned, and the Jew punished because he himself has not torn it apart, burned, or suppressed it.

In my opinion, this is legally justified: first, on the basis of the passage in [the law]: 'If someone has written, composed, or published a book to dishonour, slander, and insult someone or through malice caused this to happen, even if the book appears under another's name or anonymously, the following procedure should be adopted: The council has the authority to prosecute through the public judges and to punish this action.' To this might be added another imperial law that says: 'If anyone unwittingly comes upon a shameful and insulting book, either in his home or in the public realm or any other place, he must tear it up before anyone else may come upon it, and must not tell anyone about it. If, however, he does not immediately tear up such letters or books and burn them, but reveals the contents to another, he should know that he will be regarded as the author of this evil and suffer corporal punishment ...'

So much for invectives mentioned in the last section [i.e., section 6] on Jewish books. In this matter the action taken against a Jew should be no different from one taken against a Christian, for both [Jews and Christians] are immediate subjects of the Holy Empire and under imperial authority: we Christians through our elector, who elects the emperor, and the Jews through their own will and open admission, when they said: 'We have no king but the emperor' (John 19). Thus imperial law is binding for Christians and Jews, for each in their own proper form ...

Furthermore, according to the commission of His Imperial Majesty, my report does not extend to the 'Essrim Varba,' that is, the Twenty-four Books of the Bible, and quite rightly so, for they should be regarded as valid in every way and much respected and protected (Jerome and 2 Timn. 3: 16), for our Christian church has taken the same books into the canon as witnesses to the Truth grounded in eternity ...

[Reuchlin then goes on to discuss the Talmud. He admits that he has never read the Talmud, nor does he know any contemporary Christian who has done so. It is a collection of learned sayings and a difficult book, not easily accessible even to native Hebrew speakers.]

The Talmud is idiomatically so complex, as I said above, that not every Jew, even if he has a good command of Hebrew, can understand it. How could one therefore justify Christians rejecting the Talmud, when they cannot even understand it?

Here I would like to cite a small example. Recently a booklet appeared against the Jews,[9] in which there is a reference to a prayer in their prayer book, which they must supposedly pray especially against us Christians. It begins: ולמשמדים.[10] Great emphasis is placed on this being proof that they maliciously and venomously curse the holy apostles and their successors who have been baptized and the Christian church in general and the Roman Empire. In this manner one may easily incite hatred against the Jews among unlearned people who do not know the language, so that the Jews' lives and possessions are endangered. If one sheds further light on it, however, one finds no word in it that means 'baptized' or 'apostles' or 'Christians' or 'Roman Empire.' For משמד does not mean chrysm or baptism in any region where Hebrew is used or written. Rather it means 'destroy,' as in Proverbs 14: 'The house of the evil will be destroyed.' And Ezechiel 14: 'I shall destroy them and take them from the midst of my people Israel'; and elsewhere likewise. In this prayer, therefore, the word משמדים is a verb or active participle of the present tense and means 'destroying' or 'those who destroy them,' as if they wanted to say: Those who want to destroy us cannot hope to see their enterprise succeed.

How could it refer to 'Christians,' when there is no people in this world which deals with the Jews more liberally and shelters them as the Christians do, as can be seen in ecclesiastical and secular laws. And since the Jews, according to their voluntary declaration, have no other lord but the Christian emperor, one cannot think that such prayer was devised against the Christians. For they pray this prayer wherever they live in the world, whether it is under the regime of Turks, the Sultan, heathens, Tartars, or among us. They also know well that they would be worse off if there were no Christians, for they are more hated by heathens and receive worse treatment from them than from us.

Second, מינים means 'all those who have no right faith.' How can we tell that this refers to us rather than to others? Thirdly, קניבי means enemies, which cannot apply to us. For, as I have indicated above, we and they are co-citizens of the same Roman Empire and linked with them in citizenship and peace. How, then, can we be enemies? ... [Reuchlin continues in this vein with his analysis of the prayer, concluding:] If, then, there is no word in this prayer which, according to its precise meaning, denotes 'baptized' or 'apostle' or 'Christian' or 'Roman Empire,' why was such serious slander permitted to appear in print? One may say that the Jews had this meaning in their minds and applied these words to us in their hearts. But no one can know what is in the heart except the Creator of all hearts. Therefore no one should be reproached or punished for intentions. And if one man has such thoughts, it does not mean that another man should be subjected to punishment.

I pass over in silence other words in the same booklet, which have perhaps not been rendered correctly in German out of ignorance, as when the Jews are said to receive a Christian into their house or greet him in the street, saying 'Seit willkum'. The author of the booklet states that they say 'Sed willkum,' which according to him, means 'Devil, welcome'.[11] But according to correct usage this cannot be, for שׁד, the word for 'devil' is written with a dot on the right side of the letter 's.' For this reason it is pronounced 'sh': 'shed.' If they said 'Shed willkom' any peasant would notice that this is difference from 'Seit willkum,' for 'shed' sounds quite different from 'seit.' This is nonsense, therefore, and child's play, and need not concern us in this report.

Thus any prudent person will recognize and acknowledge that no one can reject the Talmud, who does not understand it, as the sacred ecclesiastic law says.[12] If someone wanted to write against the mathematicians and had no experience in mathematics, people would laugh at him. Similarly, if someone disputes against philosophers and has no knowledge of the teachings of philosophy. And that is what the ecclesiastic law refers to. Someone may say: 'I need not understand the Talmud, for many books have been published against the Jews in which I can read that the Talmud is evil.' Magister Raimundus says, for example, such shameful things about the Talmud in his *Pugio*[13] that respectable people don't even want to hear about it. We also read about it in the *Fortalicium fidei* and in Paulus Burgensis's *Additio* and in Brother Petrus Nigri's *Star of Messiah*.[14] And Johann Pfefferkorn, who initiated this affair, writes that the teaching of the Talmud is horrible and filthy and contains many maledictions. One might reply that no one has stated the opponent's case in an orderly and correct manner. There is a common proverb: 'One should listen to the other party as well.' Thus it is a legal principle that no one should reject or condemn anyone without first giving reasons and duly examining the matter. And even if neither party approaches the judge and demands it of him, he should nevertheless, on his own initiative, make every effort to discover and learn about the right or wrong actions of the accused party …

[In the following Reuchlin argues that it is in fact advisable to read the Talmud.] We may read good and evil writings side by side and examine them; evil writings to rectify them with prudent words, and good writings, which can be found like roses among thorns, to use them and apply them to sacred teaching. Now, there is no one who can say in truth that the Talmud, in which the four higher faculties are described, is completely evil and that one cannot learn anything good from it. For it contains many good medical prescriptions and information about plants and roots, as well as good legal verdicts collected from all over the world by experienced Jews. And in theology the Talmud offers in many passages arguments against the wrong faith. This can be seen from the bishop of Burgos's books concerning the Bible, which he has written in a praiseworthy and Christian manner, and in the *Scrutinium,* in which he clearly protects our faith on the basis of the Talmud. I noticed and counted in the first part of his *Scrutinium Scripturarum* more than fifty passages in which he draws on the Talmud for arguments against the Jews. I do not mention the other part of that book, where he points out many passages in the Talmud which support us Christians. In the preface he writes that we may learn strong and convincing arguments against the Jews from the glosses and sentences of the doctors in the Talmud, for their masters have occasionally prophesied and made predictions concerning the recondite divine mystery, although unwittingly and not knowing what they were saying, as did Caiaphas (John 11). Nevertheless the confession of the opponent is an effective proof. Thus Paulus Burgensis writes in the aforementioned preface. And he proceeds in this manner, going through the whole Bible. Wherever the Jews are against us, he argues against them on our behalf, basing his arguments on the Talmud. No one who has read his work can deny this …

[Reuchlin next argues that the Jews do not fit the category 'heretics' and can therefore not be persecuted as heretics.] Heretics are subject to the Christian church by virtue of their baptism and other sacraments they may have received; and in things concerning the faith they have no other judge but the pope and the ecclesiastics of our faith. But as far as the Jews are concerned, in matters of faith they are subject to their own judges and to no one else. No Christian should pass verdict on them, except in a secular case transacted in a secular court. For they are not members of the Christian church, and their faith is none of our business. That is also what the holy apostle Paul writes (I Cor. 5), when he says: 'Is it my business to judge the people who are on the outside? Are you not satisfied to judge those who belong to us? God will judge people who do not belong to us but stand outside ...'

[Reuchlin then turns to the Cabala.] I have read it myself. One could argue about the pros and cons for a long time in this report. But one may see from the book entitled *Apologia* by the earlier mentioned Count of Mirandola, which has been approved by Pope Alexander,[15] that the books of the Cabala are not only harmless, but of great use to the Christian faith, and Pope Sixtus IV had them translated into Latin for the use of us Christians.[16] There are sufficient grounds therefore to conclude that such books as the Cabala should not and cannot be legally suppressed and burned ...

[Concerning the Jewish glosses and commentaries, Reuchlin says]: I further claim (and can cite authorities for it) that our doctors and teachers of Holy Scripture have great need and ought to use such commentaries, glosses, and exegesis for the understanding of the biblical text, if they want to stand firm against attacks from adherents of a different faith. The holy canonical law, moreover, says that the Old Testament books should be taught with the aid of the Hebrew text.[17] And if we removed and cut out the biblical commentary of Rabbi Salomon from Nicolaus de Lyra's writings on the Bible, the remainder, that is, what Nicolaus de Lyra drew from his own mind regarding the Bible, could be contained in a few pages.[18]

Jewish commentaries should not and cannot be abandoned by the Christian church, for they keep the special characteristics of the Hebrew language before our eyes. The Bible cannot be interpreted without them, especially the Old Testament, just as we cannot do without the Greek language and Greek grammars and commentaries for the New Testament, as is confirmed and indicated in canon law. I may be permitted to add, with due respect, that there are many doctors in our Christian faith who, because they lack the knowledge of the two languages, give a defective interpretation of Sacred Scripture and expose themselves to great ridicule. Therefore one must not suppress the commentaries and glosses of authors who have learned the language from childhood on, but take care of the existing books, protect and respect them, rather than burn them, for from them flows the true meaning of the language and our understanding of Sacred Scripture ...

Furthermore, as far as their books of sermons and disputations, breviaries, songbooks, liturgy, traditions, and devotions are concerned, what else can I say but refer to the law of our praiseworthy emperor and our spiritual leader, the pope, commanding that the Jews ought to be left in peace in their synagogues, and in the exercise of ceremonies, rites, customs, habits, and devotions, especially when they do not go against what is right and do not manifestly insult our Christian church. For the Christian church has nothing to do with them, except with respect to the nine points indicated in the gloss.[19] Thus it is my opinion that the books mentioned above should in fairness not be taken, destroyed, or burned, except those that are invectives or concern forbidden arts ...

Finally, concerning the writings touching on philosophy and the liberal arts or science, which constituted point six in my arrangement, I say they should be treated as are the arts written in Greek, Latin, or German: anything not prohibited in those languages should be left intact. If there are, however, Hebrew books that teach or instruct readers in the forbidden arts, such as sorcery, magic, and witchcraft, if they may be used to harm people, they should be destroyed, torn up, and burned because they are against nature. But if such books of magic are designed only to help and benefit human life and serve no harmful purpose, one should not burn or destroy them, except books about buried treasures.[20]

Thus Your Princely Grace has my answer to the question, from which one may understand that I regard it as neither useful in glorifying God, nor in the interest of the holy Christian faith, nor in the interest of furthering devotion to tear up the books of the Jews, to suppress and burn them, with the exception of invectives, called 'libelli famosi,' and forbidden arts that are harmful to human beings and therefore not to be tolerated, as said above. For the Jews are our archivists, librarians, and antiquarians, who preserve books that can serve as witnesses to our faith ...

To come to the end of this controversy, I cannot in truth believe that any advantage can come to our Christian faith from this business or that it could serve the worship of God. Rather I can well imagine that much evil could arise from burning their writings:

1 The Jews may say that we are taking away their weapons because we are afraid that they might defeat us in disputations and surpass us in cleverness. As if a duke commanded a shepherd to fight with him, but first had the shepherd's staff, sword, or knife taken away, whereas he kept his own weapon.
2 The Jews may once again write many strange things that may be more evil than the existing ones, and tell their children in a

hundred years from now that this was written in the books that were burned.

3 They may say that our doctors were misquoting them and citing something different from what was written. In that case we would have no references to which we could take recourse.

4 What is prohibited is most popular. Their rabbis and masters would travel to Turkey to study there and return to teach their young people diligently more evil than they have learned so far.

5 It may happen, as circumstances in the world change from one year to the next, that we might urgently need these books in councils and assemblies of the church, as for example, the Council of Basel obtained the Koran, Mohammed's book, through Cardinal Johann of Ragusa.[21] Then we would give much not to have burned them, as happened to the Romans, when King Tarquinius Priscus burned the books of Sibylla Amalthea, except for the last three, for which he had to pay three hundred gold pieces, much regretting that he had burned the others.[22]

6 We are prohibited from disputing publicly with heretics who have abandoned our faith. But we are allowed to debate with Jews and talk with them to convert them to our faith. If their books are burned, how could we support our arguments against them, except on the basis of their text of the Bible? …

The canonical law commands us not to deprive the Jews of their possessions, cash or goods of monetary value, that is, goods covered under the term *pecunia*. Anyone who acts contrary to this law is deprived of his office and titles and banned (or, excommunicated) until he offers compensation. It is a legal principle that no one is banned unless he has committed a capital sin. If it is a sin, it cannot serve to glorify God. This commandment of the church goes for all kings and the emperor insofar as they are Christians. And the imperial law has taken over the canonical law … and as long as the Jews keep the peace, they ought to be left in peace. And all this must be observed so that they cannot say that they are being forced and compelled to convert to our faith …

Since our gracious lord, the Roman emperor, has asked for my counsel, I cannot give him better advice than to say to his Imperial Majesty: For the sake of God and our Christian faith he should give directions that the universities in Germany should hire for the next ten years two lecturers each, who would be capable and have the task of teaching students Hebrew and instructing them in this language, as the Clementine decree points out and directs us to do.[23] In this undertaking the Jews resident in our region should kindly aid us by lending us their books, against an appropriate guarantee that they should not be damaged, until we have obtained our own through copying or printing. If this is done, I doubt not that in a few years our students will be so well versed in the Hebrew language that they will be able to bring the Jews over to our side with reasonable and friendly words and gentle means, following the direction of the canonical law, which expressly says: 'Whoever has the genuine intention of leading persons unfamiliar with the Christian religion to the right faith, must do so with gentle words and must not begin in a harsh spirit, lest they be alienated, when they might be turned from their erroneous path through good reasoning.'

**Notes**

1 For a modern, critical edition of the *Eye Mirror* see *Johann Reuchlin. Sämtliche Werke*, ed. W.-W. Ehlers et al. (Stuttgart-Bad Cannstatt 1999), vol. 4–1, 13–168.
2 Uriel of Gemmingen, archbishop of Mainz, 1508–14
3 Maximilian I (1459–1519) was emperor from 1493 to 1519. On the imperial commission see above, pp. 10–11.
4 The famous medieval exegete David Kimchi, whom Reuchlin cites repeatedly, distinguished *perush* from *derashot*. The latter were homiletic interpretations of the Bible; the former were commentaries conforming to the standards of *peshat*, the rigorous examination of the literal and historical meaning of the bible.
5 Midrashic literature offers allegorical interpretations of the Bible; for *derashot* ('draschut' in Reuchlin's transliteration), see preceding note.
6 I.e., the *Nizzachon* (Victory) written by Rabbi Jomtop Lipmann in 1399. Reuchlin was given a copy of the book in 1494. See above, chapter 4, n. 13. *Toldot Jeshu ha Nozri* was a biography of Jesus considered slanderous by Christians. Cf. S. Krauss, ed. *Toldot Yeshu: Das Leben Jesu nach jüdischen Quellen* (Hildesheim, 1977).
7 Paul of Burgos (Salomon ben Levi, before his conversion to Christianity; 1351–1435) wrote a commentary on the Bible, entitled *Scrutinium Scripturarum* (Scrutiny of Scripture) and *Additiones* (Additions) to Lyra's commentary.
8 Cf above, p. 15.
9 I.e., Pfefferkorn's *Enemy of the Jews*, see above, Document 1.
10 See above, p. 55. The word is, in fact, passive and means 'destroyed' and, metaphorically, 'converted.' I.e., a person who has abandoned the Jewish faith is, in the eyes of the Jews, 'destroyed.'

11 Cf. Document 1, p. 56. Reuchlin's spelling of the German phrase differs from Pfefferkorn's, but the sound effect is the same.

12 Gratian, *Decretum*, 1.37.11

13 The theologian Raimundus Martini (1220–86), Spanish Hebraist, perhaps a Jewish convert. He wrote the *Pugio fidei* (The knife [i.e., a defensive weapon] of faith).

14 For the *Fortalicium fidei* and Nigri's book, see above, p. 8. On Paul of Burgos see above, n. 5.

15 The papal brief appears on the verso of the title page of Pico's *Opera Omnia* vol. 1 (Basel, 1572; repr. Turin, 1971).

16 See above, p. 16.

17 Gratian, *Decretum*, I.9.6

18 Nicolaus of Lyra (1270–1349) wrote an extensive commentary on the Bible, known as *Postilla*. He used the work of Rabbi Salomon ben Isaak (Raschi). Lyra's work was corrected and expanded by Paul of Burgos in the *Additamenta* or *Additiones* (Additions).

19 I.e., the gloss on Pope Gregory IX's decretals 5.6.5.

20 As dictated by imperial law, Codex Iustinianus 10.15.1.

21 Cardinal John of Ragusa (Johannes Stoichowic) attended the Council of Basel (1431–49). He died there, leaving his books to the Dominicans in Basel. Reuchlin had one copy of the Greek New Testament on permanent loan.

22 The story of Tarquinius Priscus is told by Lactantius, *Institutiones*, 1.6.101.

23 The decree of Pope Clement V based on the decisions made at the Council of Vienne (1312), which recommends that universities teach Hebrew, Syrian, and Arabic to train future missionaries.

DOCUMENT 4

# Johann Reuchlin

## *Defence against the Cologne Slanderers*

The following translation is based on the text entitled in Latin *Defensio contra calumniatores suos Colonienses* (Tübingen, 1513). It is addressed to Emperor Maximilian I, since Reuchlin took the position that the report (Document 3) condemned by the Cologne theologians had been a confidential document meant for the emperor's eyes only and that Pfefferkorn had made some of its contents public contrary to imperial law and on the instigation of the Cologne theologians. The aggressive tone of Reuchlin's *Defence* differs sharply from his polite exchanges with the faculty during the previous year, when he was still hoping to forestall a condemnation (see above, pp. 18–19). A critical edition of the Latin text with a German translation can be found in *Johann Reuchlin: Sämtliche Werke*, ed. W.-W. Ehlers et al. (Stuttgart-Bad Cannstatt, 1999), IV–1: 197–443. The passages translated are on pp. 202–26, 234–8, 260, 380–4, 442.

### *Defence against the Cologne Slanderers*

I put my trust in you, august Emperor, as I respond with alacrity and clarity to the atrocious, immense, and unprecedented insults and injuries to a man who is your councillor and a veteran courtier of your saintly father.[1] Contrary to everything that is right and lawful, a group of Cologne professors has published these vehement insults in slanderous pamphlets.[2] As I hear, they have been disseminated in a thousand copies and, having been read by practically everyone, have finally been brought before Your Majesty. Thus you and the whole world, whose governor and ruler you are, may not only regard them with your eyes but also, as it were, touch the deceitful and fraudulent words themselves with your hands and restore to me my well deserved reputation, and a more fortunate one. I am obliged to deal here with boors who are more intent on fighting than finding the truth, and I speak in a thinly textured style of which I am ashamed. It is a barren and jejune style lacking rhetorical ornaments and devoid of any elegance worthy of Your Majesty's ears, which are used to a sweeter tune, but I must adapt my poor speech to those trifling sophists and make my case artlessly, almost ungrammatically, as my speech winds its way to the end of the business through thorny thickets and paths full of briars. I must speak in this manner to make it easier for my opponents to understand me, for they are otherwise cunning blusterers,[3] but their speech is rustic and barbarous; they are inexperienced in the Latin language and disgusted with humanistic studies ...

Three years ago, best and greatest emperor, I received with due respect a mandate from Your Most Holy Majesty, an official communication written in German, included and properly sealed in letters, also in German, from your Most Illustrious Arch-Chancellor Uriel of Gemmingen, archbishop of Mainz,[4] in which he urged me, in virtue of the commission given to him by you, to obey your commands and precepts forthwith and without delay. According to the tenor of the mandate I was asked to give my considered opinion and to counsel Your Majesty concerning the destruction of all Jewish books (with the sole exception of the Bible); whether the collection or burning of all Jewish books except the Bible would contribute to the glory of God and the welfare of Christendom, and the increase of devotion. Joining in your request, the prince exhorted me to send my opinion to him as quickly and promptly as possible, that he might execute your commission. You had given him instructions to collect the opinions of all advisors named by you, to give them his full consideration, and transmit them to Your Majesty together with his own opinion. When I had read the letters and your saintly decree, I confess I was struck dumb at first. I did not know what you wanted to do, what your purpose and intention was, whether you wanted to burn books which, according to dependable historical documents, generally accepted annals, and other trustworthy sources, no Roman emperor from the beginning to the end of recorded time has ever thought of burning. I could not find any passage either in sacred scripture or in civil law, nothing in the ecclesiastic sanctions or determinations of the universal church or the decrees of the holy Fathers, in which there was a verdict about actually burning the books of the Jews or deliberating such action ...

I answered the question [concerning the Jewish books] in these words: If there is any Jew who knowingly owns a book that was written expressly, simply, and plainly to defame, blaspheme, and speak scandalously or irreverently against our Lord Jesus, his most worthy mother, the saints, or the Christian constitutions and degrees, that book could be confiscated and burned by imperial mandate, and the Jew himself could be punished because he himself had neglected to tear up the book, burn, and suppress it ... [Reuchlin sums up the remainder of his report].

When my counsel was in the hands of your arch-chancellor, the most illustrious prince, and before it was presented to Your Majesty, a baptized Jew from Cologne by name of Pfefferkorn, calling himself 'enemy of the Jews,' a no-good man, or rather a poisonous beast, managed somehow by fraudulent means, by deceit and evil intent, and through perfidious people, to anticipate you and obtain your report (I say 'your' because it was written for your attention, on your command, and given to your representative). He was furious because he saw that it was my opinion that not all of the Jewish writings should be destroyed, which is the revenge he wanted and in which he was aided by many with the most iniquitous and unjust counsel. He made my report known to the public through numerous transcriptions ... Not satisfied with divulging it, not remaining within these limits, not stopping at this crime, that Jew sprinkled with water went further. Disdaining the law, cheating on social custom, turning away from Christian charity, instructed by men who boast of being doctors, and supplied by them with many and various useless quotations, this man who is ignorant of theology and law, inexperienced in literature, and knowing no book written in the Latin language, equipped only with some childish, trite Jewish stuff, undertook to write against me and published a slanderous book in German, full of invented charges. Like a crude fellow who does not care about his reputation or honour or good name, he ventured it, armed with audacity, took risks like a dead man exposing himself to death, against whom one cannot fight except with the help of ghosts. He is a man, by his own judgment, unworthy to be taken on by any good and serious-minded man. Well then, this past April, 1511, his slanderous book made its appearance in Frankfurt. It was entitled *Hand Mirror*, stitched together against me out of the machinations of those pseudo-scholars, published under the name of the traitor. Some thousand copies were published by a printer in Mainz.[5] Pfefferkorn himself indicated clearly in his prologue the authors of the deed, he is used to betraying others and, like a leaky vessel, could not keep it in or conceal that most cursed faction of men. Rather, he names in the preface of his libellous book a certain Arnold of Tungern,[6] who was chosen by his colleagues on the theological faculty to act against me, as he himself attests. It was therefore necessary to make an attempt to counter with the truth whatever it was this bold man had written against me and to correct the rumours. I diligently set about to do what I had decided and which I was obliged to do: I saw to it that the truth won out, and I called my apologia in the German language *Augenspiegel*, 'Eye Mirror,' because the slanderer had called his book 'Hand Mirror.' It was a more auspicious title, I think, because the eye (not the hand) has sight, and I am displaying my innocence to the eyes, whereas he offers his slanders to the hands, that is, to violence. For he himself wanted to use his hands against me ... Thus I have decided to expose his evil words to the mirror of the eye, that all good men may clearly and manifestly see that my adversaries have used more than thirty-four lies in the *Hand Mirror* to bring shame on me. To make their inventions clearer than the sun, I wished to point out each lie. This, however, would not have been possible without publishing the counsel I gave you, Most August Emperor, which had been first divulged and published by the traitor. I published it for all to see, so that the whole German nation could recognize the deceitfulness of that slanderer by means of signs placed on each page.[7] Thus I was obliged on account of this great risk to my reputation and in defence of my welfare to publish the report myself and expose it to the eyes of the man in the street, to any reader, worthy or unworthy. I knew of course that I might be attacked and get involved in discussions with ignorant and malicious men, who are perhaps not as respectfully disposed toward a man whom they do not know as you are toward me, my emperor, for you have a good opinion of me and have seen proof of my honesty. And for this reason I added to the report a scholarly disputation with brief arguments to refute [any accusations], so that scholars and learned men might recognize that I think just as the Catholic church thinks. And I said so expressly in my report, professing my integrity and sincere faith ...

[All of Reuchlin's friends were pleased with his book, which restored his reputation, but the supporters of Pfefferkorn were displeased that the truth had overcome their false arguments.] One of them, the people's priest in Frankfurt (*plebanus*, as they call the office),[8] assumed the role of the representative of Mainz[9] and forbade the booksellers to sell the volume containing my defence. He had read it to Pfefferkorn, the baptized Jew, as he sat by his side eating dinner with him, and, if I recall correctly, in the presence of Pfefferkorn's wife, a good-looking woman who usually joins her husband around town, at home or when they are invited. That priest reported the reason for his interference (the false reason, rather) to the archbishop, but the most illustrious prince who was already convinced that I had been done a great injury, did not want to prohibit the sale of my apologia since he had not prohibited the slanderous book. Indeed he refused to confirm the prohibition, for he knew that it was unjust and spiteful. When, therefore, the magistrate gave permission for the sale of my apologia, the *Eye Mirror*, more copies were sold than before, so that 'this Codrus[10] burst his spleen.' Irked by this and piqued by anger, the priest, that little mass-sayer, proclaimed from the pulpit before all the people congregated at mass that Pfefferkorn, the baptized Jew, would preach in his place on the following feast day of the Most Blessed Virgin Mary, and urged them to come in great numbers. For now the wretched Pfefferkornians were tormented by the thought that none of their writings had succeeded in shaking my renown and reputation, and so with malice prepense they created an opportunity for criticizing and slandering me behind my back (such backhanded tricks never even entered my mind); under the pretext of giving a sermon they wanted to denigrate my name and make me hateful to the people, so that they might achieve by word of mouth and without me hearing it what they could not achieve with their writings. And behold, at the appointed time, the notorious Pfefferkorn came, with great sanctity (O God and saints above!) or rather full of evil hypocrisy; 'with bent head and lowered eyes, mumbling (but keeping in his heart a wrathful silence), he opened his lips and weighed his words,'[11] looking like one praying and making vows. Then that Jew, baptized with water, rose up in the church, a married layman, before the congregation of faithful, that is, before the assembled church, and preached about the word of God and the Christian faith in an authoritative manner, he – a butcher and an ignoramus – blessed the people with the sign of the cross ... [Reuchlin notes that this is against the law of the church and cites the pertinent injunctions]. I am not concerned about the injury done to me, my emperor, as long as you and all Christians are most concerned about the indignity done to the church. That standard-bearer of the Cologne professors dared to post his sermon on the notice board and at the pulpit, a crime, for which in my time and memory a simple peasant, a farm worker in Niclashausen, was condemned and burned at the stake, although he was misled by a nocturnal vision in the fields, and was not known as underhanded or motivated by greed. But Pfefferkorn was not deceived by a dream or by demons and ghosts, which he himself calls 'lullos' (a corrupt word coming out of his corrupt and putrid mouth),[12] not moved or persuaded, not misled by his simplicity. He did not err out of piety, but was taught by the shallowest hypocrites, by cheaters and pretenders, the professors who have been overcome by cupidity and avarice. Instructed and suborned by them, a bad disciple of bad teachers, fully aware, willingly and knowingly, he perpetrated many great crimes, many wicked deeds, many intolerable acts against divine and human law, machinating against the precepts and instructions and legal statutes in his native audacity, temerity, and fury ...

[It is not the first time that theologians have conspired to ruin scholars.] In our own time Filelfo was derided as 'philelcus'[13] and the most learned Giovanni Pico, count of Mirandola,[14] was miserably harassed by rivals, not to mention Sebastian Brant,[15] a doctor of law, learned in the best disciplines, and well known for the integrity of his life, who was attacked and torn to pieces by Brother Vigandus, a Dominican; not to mention the learned jurist Peter of Ravenna[16] being falsely accused by some Cologne theologians, as he says in the apologetic writings published in recent years; not to mention myself being unjustly attacked by the Cologne 'theologists.' In this manner good men have always suffered at the hands of bad men, but with the passage of time the slander recoils on the heads of the authors, while the harassed men recover their good name and reputation which by law should never have been harmed. Thus my adversaries are rendered notorious and infamous by their own actions and cannot, even if they make a great effort, actually slander me or anyone else before good and grave men. Neither their words nor their writings nor their testimony against others carry weight, for they are unworthy of all honour and lack any real credibility and command no respect either here or elsewhere. For who would believe them or expect any truth from them? They have been made soft and malleable by their flawed condition, they are lighter than a feather or lighter than Epicurean atoms.[17] I cannot call my Cologne slanderers theologians; they are false theologians ... and I shall call them from now on by a term of reproach 'theologists' because I do not want to anger anyone in the saintly assembly of true theologians at other universities ...

[The Cologne slanderers] are puffed up with human learning, do not blush to live a lie and speak lies, are interested only in contentious, quarrelsome disputations, for which they arm their tongues, and have long abandoned good deeds. There is a great void,[18] a great sinkhole, as is very well known, between theologians and theologists, as big a difference as between virtue and vice, good and bad, genuine and counterfeit, true and false. Yet they are all called, without distinction, by the common name 'theologians.' But if we weigh and measure prudently the nature, condition, character, and deeds of each group, we may conclude without a doubt that one group can be called theologians in actual fact, the others only by a fancy ...

[There was no need for the Cologne theologians to proceed against him in this aggressive manner.] Even if my report had been irreligious, scandalous, and offensive to the ears of pious people, I should not have been slandered as if I were a heathen, as if I were unwilling to listen to the church once I was informed of the matter. The report could have been ground into the earth, thrown into the fire, submerged in a river before that traitor Pfefferkorn, that triple-thief, published the confidential and sealed document without your knowledge, before he published his slanderous tractate against me, which was full of and replete with puerile quotations from the law and from theology – and this from a man who knows no books and was a short while ago an ignorant butcher but has now become a sack-carrier in a mill and a weigher of salt[19] for the men from Cologne. And he dedicated his book to Arnold [Tungern], the rector of the bursa[20] ...

I wrote about a matter that had not yet been determined by the church, about burning the books of the Jews, and wrote what I thought, submitting myself to the judgment of the church and writing in the belief that the church had said nothing to the contrary. I did so without being guilty of carelessness, searching for the hidden truth with every kind of argument, but without prejudice to anyone who knew better, and I was prepared to correct anything, if I was shown that the church held a different belief. I even asked to be corrected. Yet no one has in truth demonstrated any error and it is certain that I am free of guilt and have committed no culpable deed. Indeed I have not sinned, and I am not sinning now. I believe that I have in my published and printed declarations rebutted over and over again those silly sophisms of my Cologne slanderers and their senile arguments which are based on lies and injustice. For they are not true theologians whom one must believe, they are not worthy of the great and precious name of theology. They do not act like theologians but like jesters, like shameful blatherers, like notorious actors and detractors, who bring wrong accusations against innocent men and attempt to denigrate my name with seditious sermons, although I am innocent and have taken great care never to harm them in any way. They attempt to arouse hatred against me and in this manner to win a little glory among inexperienced men. If they were truly theologians or true theologians, they would have been obliged to argue against my positions (if I had asserted or held any such positions) either from the lectern or in the public arena, in an academic fashion, that is, to fight with reasons, not with insults, to dispute with statements according to the respectable custom of all other universities and in the praiseworthy manner of France, Italy, and Germany. I would have accepted this patiently, for opposing views arise among the doctors every day, and there are divisions in the schools, and each doctor battles against the rational argumentation of another according to his own understanding and rationale, without detriment to the academic community and without causing a rift. But no good man, no man of integrity who is worthy of living and breathing the air, no one to be tolerated among human beings, has descended to this level of frivolity and injustice that he passes judgment without judgment and condemns without jurisdiction and proscribes without authority. Such are my opponents, not just geese whose honking is harmless, but dogs who bark and bite. These Cologne theologists, my slanderers, are hell hounds,[21] they are infernal furies! …

[Reuchlin next defends his report against the aspersions of Arnold Tungern.][22] No one ever heard me say, nor have I affirmed orally or in writing that the Jews have a right to propagate every one of the books of the Talmud. No, I have said the opposite, [excepting] in the first part of my report books that are blasphemous and insulting, and in the last part, books about magic. How can Arnold be called a logical thinker or a logician? He does not understand the nature of opposites, for he says that these two propositions are opposed to one another and cannot both be valid, one being 'I have read many books and have found no disrespect in any,' and the second being 'There are many blasphemies and heresies in the books of the Jews.' Although I have not in fact phrased it in this manner, I am surprised nevertheless at his denial that both propositioins may be valid at the same time. From this it is clear that Arnold is neither a philosopher nor a doctor of theology, unless he is a doctor created from nothing, for they sometimes create such doctors.[23] For this reason, my emperor, do not expect from that quarter anything firm, constant, strong, theological, or even worthy of a philosopher. You will find nothing in him except soft, effeminate, puerile, awkward stuff, hesitations and doubt. For he is as timid as a hare. He dares affirm nothing in his argumentation. He does not dare to say A=B. He is like a monkey who stretches out his hand, when asked, then retracts it out of fear, for he always meditates deceit in his mind. For this reason he starts almost all his arguments with 'as it seems,' 'it appears,' 'one might suspect,' 'it may be divined,' 'apparently,' 'I believe,' 'he appears to want,' 'these words appear to smack of heresy,' 'as far as I can make out, this or that is not pertinent,' 'he appears to cite inappropriately.' It is up to your judgment, my emperor, whatever strikes you as pertinent or not pertinent, for you are an impartial judge. Throughout his slanderous book that 'quasi-man' does not dare to deny or affirm anything without using the adverb *quasi* [so to speak]. Like a man hypnotized, he repeats *quasi, quasi, quasi,* he wants to hint at this – so to speak, wishes to say – so to speak, in a public matter – so to speak, as if there can be no worry about anything else – so to speak ... By making me ignominious, he was hoping to transmit his name to posterity for ever, hoping that he would be given a golden statue by the theologists on account of his wonderful skill in maligning me. I am not so envious of another man's glory that I do not concede to my adversary the ample, illustrious, and shining honour of a lasting monument, which he strives for with such superlative ambition. Certainly I shall not prevent him from boasting four names to perpetuate his memory, as was customary among noble Romans, a first name, a middle name, a family name, and an epithet. Let him seek a splendid title for himself even on the basis of suppressing mine. Indeed I shall even help him if I can. This slanderer or rather slaughterer of my name has my permission to call himself before all nations and coming generations, starting this very 1st of March, 1513, by the following four notable, illustrious, and glorious names and carve them in cedar or boxwood or marble, if he wants: Arnold Tungern Slanderer Cheater, for ever and ever.

**Notes**

1 Frederick III, emperor from 1440 to 1493.
2 I.e., Reuchlin assumes that the Cologne theologians were behind Pfefferkorn's publications. See below, n. 6.
3 'Cunning blusterers' translates *vulpiones et bovinatores*. The meaning of the Latin expressions is uncertain, but the words are obviously related to *vulpis* (fox) and *bos* (bull).
4 Uriel of Gemmingen, archbishop of Mainz (1508–74), was chancellor by virtue of his office. As one of the seven electors (officials who elected the

emperor) he was also a prince of the Empire and is addressed by this title.

5 The book was printed by Johann Schöffer.

6 The *Hand Mirror* was dedicated to Tungern. See Böcking, *Supplementum*, II:75.

7 I.e., placing letters in the margin of the edition which pointed the reader to Reuchlin's rebuttals.

8 Petrus Meyer, *plebanus* at St Bartholomew's in Frankfurt.

9 Frankfurt was in the diocese and under the jurisdiction of the archbishop of Mainz. Meyer acted as if he were the representative of the archbishop of Mainz.

10 Codrus, a bad poet who envied and attacked the great poet Virgil. The phrase is a quotation from Virgil, *Eclogues*, 7:26.

11 A quotation from the Roman satirist Persius, *Satires*, 3.80–82.

12 Reuchlin himself uses the proper words for ghosts: *larvae* and *lemures*.

13 Francesco Filelfo (1398–1481), renowned Italian humanist and popular university teacher; his satires gave offence to some members of the church. 'Philelcus' is an invented compound. The prefix *phil* means 'fond of'; 'elcus' may be derived from *helkos* (=wound); i.e., Filfelfo is 'fond of wounding' others.

14 See above, p. 15.

15 Sebastian Brant (1457–1521), by profession a jurist but best known as the author of the satirical *Ship of Fools* (1494). He was attacked by the Dominican Vigandus because of his writings about the immaculate conception of St Mary.

16 Peter of Ravenna, an Italian jurist teaching at the University of Cologne. His views on the burial of criminals were attacked by theologians who contended that he had trespassed on their professional territory. Jacob Hoogstraten, who prosecuted Reuchlin, had written tracts against Peter of Ravenna in 1508 and 1511. The jurist was obliged to leave Cologne.

17 Epicurus (d. 270 BC) was an exponent of the ancient atomist philosophy.

18 Reuchlin uses the term *chaos*, but this may be a misprint for *chasma*, chasm.

19 *Saccularius* (sack-carrier) can also mean 'purse snatcher.' Reuchlin may have used this ambiguous term deliberately, alluding to the allegations that Pfefferkorn was a thief (see above, p. 3). A *salipensor*, or measurer of salt, supervised the buying of salt from the public warehouse. This was one of Pfefferkorn's duties as a warden at the Dominicans' hospital. The references to his thieving and his position as measurer of salt also appear in one of the *Letters of Obscure Men* (I.36). The fictitious writer relates a conversation between himself and unnamed enemies of Pfefferkorn:

'They said: That Johann Pfefferkorn of yours in Cologne is one of the worst buffoons. He knows no Hebrew and became a Christian only to hide his criminal deeds ... Once gallows were set up to have him hanged for theft, but he made his escape one way or another ... Then I was angry and replied: You lie in your throats, you vile Jews! ... Pfefferkorn is as good and zealous a Christian as anyone in Cologne ... Do you think that our professors and the mayor of Cologne were stupid, when they made him warden of the major hospital and a measurer of salt? They would not have done it if he was not a good Catholic.'

20 Arnold Tungern (d. 1540), professor of theology at the University of Cologne, and for some years in charge of one of the *bursae,* or student residences. He was delegated by the faculty to examine Reuchlin's *Eye Mirror* and published the resulting *Articles and Propositions concerning suspicions of [Reuchlin] favouring the Jews* in 1512.

21 Literally 'Cerberuses,' a reference to Cerberus, the mythological dog who guards the Underworld.

22 See above, n. 6.

23 Reuchlin is thinking of doctorates granted *per saltum,* that is, without fulfilling the academic requirements. Honorary doctorates are the modern equivalent.

## DOCUMENT 5

# *Letters of Obscure Men*

The following texts are translations from the *Epistolae obscurorum virorum*, which appeared anonymously and without place of publication. The book was likely printed in Cologne in 1515. It contained forty-one fictitious letters, addressed to Ortwin Gratius (see above, p. 20) and was published on the initiative of the Erfurt humanist Crotus Rubeanus (1480–1545), who wrote most of the letters in this volume. Crotus studied at the Universities of Erfurt and Cologne, and then travelled to Italy, where he obtained a doctorate of theology from the University of Bologna (1517). He became an enthusiastic Lutheran, was appointed chancellor to Duke Albert of Brandenburg and was instrumental in introducing Protestantism in Prussia. In 1530, however, he returned to the Catholic faith and entered the service of the archbishop of Mainz. He was denounced as a traitor by his Lutheran friends, but continued his career in the Catholic church.

Another edition of the *Epistolae obscurorum virorum*, with an appendix of seven letters, most of them written by Ulrich von Hutten, appeared in the fall of 1516. The new letters mix political with academic concerns. In the original edition the fictitious letter-writers had made-up names, such as 'Plumilegus' (Feather-gatherer), 'Genselinus' (Gooser), 'Mellilambius' (Honey-licker). The letters in the appendix are attributed to historical persons (Hoogstraten, Tungern). Hutten (1488–1523), descendant of a family of imperial knights, was a talented poet and satirist. He was crowned poet laureate by Emperor Maximilian in 1517. An early supporter of Luther, he was prepared to use violent means to assure the success of the Reformation. He was motivated primarily by patriotic feelings and the belief that the corrupt Roman court was exploiting Germany. Until 1520 he enjoyed the patronage of the archbishop of Mainz, but his violent temper soon lost him the archbishop's favour. Lutherans, too, were wary of his methods. He found a new patron in the condottiere Franz von Sickingen and enjoyed his protection when he embarked on the so-called *Pfaffenkrieg* (war against the clergy). When Sickingen was killed in action, Hutten fled to Basel and Zurich, where he died of syphilis.

In the spring of 1517 a third much enlarged, edition of the *Epistolae* appeared. It contained a second book, or section, with sixty-two letters. These were substantially the contribution of Hutten and reflect his belligerent temper. Some of the letters were added by Hermann Buschius (1468–1534), who looked after the publication of the 1517 edition. Buschius, a wandering scholar, had spent some ten years in Italy, studying at Rome and in Bologna. For a while he taught poetry at the University of Cologne, but in 1502 he moved to the newly founded University of Wittenberg. The next year he taught at the University of Leipzig, from which he was however ousted for his blustering and insulting behaviour. He met Crotus Rubeanus in Erfurt, from where he was expelled under similar circumstances. He became a champion of Luther and, between 1527 and 1533, taught at the first reformed university in Marburg. He was a well-respected poet and an effective promoter of the Reformation.

The fictitious letters are written in pidgin Latin to lampoon the language of the scholastics. They contain many exaggerations and inventions that border on slander, as is to be expected from satire. The following translations are based on the Latin text edited by Griffin Stokes (London 1909). Stokes also provided an English translation which reproduces the awkwardness of the pidgin Latin (reprinted in *On the Eve of the Reformation*, with an introduction by H. Holborn, New York, 1964). I have opted for plain English. The numbering of the letters indicates the section and the number of the letter in that section.

## *Letters of Obscure Men*

### I.2 From Magister Johannes Pellifex to Magister Ortwin Gratius

Friendly greetings and incredibly slavish devotion! Reverend Herr Magister, as Aristotle says in his *Praedicamenta*, it is useful to have doubts about specific points.[1] Therefore I want to tell you of a matter that is weighing heavily on my conscience. Recently I was at the Frankfurt [book] Fair, and as I was walking along the street with a certain Bachelor, we encountered two men, who, to all outward appearance, were reputable men. They wore black cassocks and great hoods with flaps. Now, heaven be my witness, I took them for two Doctors of Theology, and I greeted them, taking off my cap. Immediately the Bachelor nudged me, and said, 'By the love of God! What are you doing? Those fellows are Jews, and you have taken off your cap to them!' At this I was as terrified as if I had seen the devil. And I said, 'Herr Bachelor, may the Lord forgive me, for I did it out of ignorance. But what do you think, was it a great sin?' And at first he said that in his view it was a mortal sin,[2] inasmuch as it fell under the category of idolatry and broke the first commandment, 'Believe in one God.' He said: 'When any one pays respect to a Jew or a heathen as though he were a Christian, he goes against Christianity and seems to be a Jew or pagan himself. Then the Jews and pagans will say: Aha! Ours is the better way, for the Christians bow to us. And unless ours was the better way, they would not bow to us. And thus they are confirmed in their own belief and despise the Christian faith and refuse to be baptized.' I replied: 'That's true enough if the sin is committed knowingly, but I did it in ignorance, and ignorance excuses sin. For if I had known that they were Jews and had nevertheless taken off my cap, then I would deserve to be burned at the stake for heresy. But, heaven knows, I had no idea from anything they said or did that they were Jews. I thought they were Doctors.' But he insisted it was a sin nevertheless, and he added: 'I myself was once in a church, where I saw a wooden statue of a Jew before the Saviour, grasping a hammer. I mistook it for a statue of St Peter with a key, and I genuflected and took off my cap. Then I saw that it was meant to be a Jew, and I immediately repented. But when I went to confession in the Dominican monastery, the confessor told me that the sin was mortal because we must always be on guard, and he told me he could not have absolved me, if he did not have an episcopal licence, for it was a case for the bishop.[3] And he said, if I had done it willingly and not out of ignorance, it would have been a case for the pope. And so I was absolved, because he had an episcopal licence. And, by God, I think that if you want to save your soul, you ought to confess to the proper official. Ignorance cannot excuse that sin, because you should have been on the lookout, and the Jews always wear a round yellow patch on their cloaks in front, which you could have seen as well as I.[4] Therefore it was crass ignorance and does not excuse the sin.' That's what the Bachelor said to me. But you are a profound theologian, and I ask you humbly and devoutly to solve this question for me and tell me whether this sin is mortal or venial, whether the aforesaid is an ordinary or an episcopal or a papal case. And also write and tell me if, in your opinion, it is right for the citizens of Frankfurt to have a dress code that allows Jews to walk around in the garb of Doctors of Theology. It seems to me that it is not right, that it is a great scandal that there should not be an obvious distinction between Jews and Doctors. It is a mockery of holy theology. His Serene Highness the Emperor ought not to permit a Jew, who is a dog and an enemy of Christ, to walk around like a Doctor of holy Theology ... Farewell, in the name of the Lord.

I.5 From Johannes Straussfederius to Ortwin Gratius

Superlative health and as many good nights as there are stars in the sky and fish in the sea! I want you to know that both I and my mother are in good health. And I would like to hear the same of you, for I think of Your Lordship at least once a day. But with your permission, let me tell you about the incredible behaviour of a certain nobleman here.[5] May the Devil confound him to the end of his days, for he insulted Herr Magister Peter Meyer[6] at dinner in the presence of many gentlemen and noblemen. He showed not a bit of respect. I was amazed at his arrogance. 'Look,' he said, 'Doctor Reuchlin is more learned than you,' and he snapped his fingers at him. Then Magister Peter replied: 'I'll be hanged if that is true. Holy Mary! Doctor Reuchlin is a mere child in theology – a child knows more theology than Doctor Reuchlin. Holy Mary! Mark my words, for I have experience, whereas he knows nothing about the *Book of Sentences*.[7] Holy Mary! Now that's subtle stuff for you. You can't pick that up as easily as grammar or poetry. I could be a good poet and even know how to compose metric verse, for I have taken a course in Leipzig about Sulpitius's *Quantities of Syllables*.[8] So what gives? Let him propose a question in theology and argue for and against it.' And he gave many reasons why no one was a perfect theologian, unless inspired by the Holy Spirit. It was the Holy Spirit who imbued a man with this skill. Poetry, however, was the food of the devil, as Jerome says in his epistle.[9] But that buffoon said it was not true, and that Doctor Reuchlin too had the Holy Spirit, enough spirit for theology, for he composed a very theological book – I don't know what it is called – and he called Magister Meyer a beast and swore that Professor Hoogstraten was nothing but a cheese-begging friar,[11] and the whole table was roaring with laughter. But I said it was shameful that a mere student should behave with such lack of respect toward a doctor of divinity. And Doctor Peter was so incensed that he rose from the table and cited the gospel,[11] saying: 'You are a Samaritan and possessed by the devil!' And I said: 'Take that!' and was very pleased that he had truly expedited that buffoon.

You must proceed in your actions and must defend theology as you have before and you must have no regard for anyone, nobleman or peasant, for you are qualified sufficiently yourself. If I could make poems like you, I wouldn't care even about a prince, even if he wanted to kill me. I am an enemy of the jurists for they walk around in red boots and furs, and do not pay enough respect to the professors. And I beg you humbly and lovingly to indicate to me how matters stand in Paris concerning the *Eye Mirror*. May God give that our august mother, the University of Paris, side with you and burn that heretical book, for it contains much scandal, as our Professor Tungern wrote[12] ... May you live a hundred years. And farewell in peace. At Mainz.

I.17 From Magister Johannes Hipp to Magister Ortwin Gratius

'Rejoyce in the Lord and you who are just be exultant, and let us all glory, who are of the right heart' (Ps. 31:11). Do not worry yourself and say: 'What does this man want with his quotation?' You will be glad when you read the following news, which will gladden Your Lordship wonderfully; and I'll write it in a few words. There was a poet here, by name of Johannes Aesticampianus,[13] an arrogant fellow, always disdainful of the masters of arts and putting them down in his lectures. He said they were inept and that one poet was worth ten masters, and that poets should always take precedence over masters and [theological] licentiates in academic processions. He lectured on Pliny and other poets[14] and declared that the masters were not masters of the seven liberal arts but of the seven deadly sins, and they did not have basic skills because they did not know the poets and only knew Peter of Spain and the *Parva Logicalia*.[15] And he had many students attending his lectures and many boarders. And he said that the Scotists and Thomists[16] had nothing to offer, and he uttered blasphemies against the Holy Doctor.[17] The professors waited their time, planning to avenge themselves with the help of God. And it was God's will that he should make a speech that scandalized the professors, doctors, licentiates, and bachelors. In the speech he praised his faculty and insulted holy theology. There was a great deal of indignation among the heads of the faculty. And the masters and doctors held a consultation, saying: 'What shall we do? This man has done many well-known things. If we send him away, people will say it's because he is more learned than we. The moderns will come and say that their way is better than the old way, and our university will be vilified, and there will be a great scandal.' Then Magister Andreas Delitsch,[18] who is a fine poet himself, said that in his opinion Aesticampianus was needed at the university like a fifth wheel on a wagon. He thwarted the other faculties and kept students from qualifying for the examination. The other masters swore that this was the case. In short, they decided either to expel that poet or to prevent him from lecturing, at the risk of his everlasting resentment. And so they cited him before the rector and posted the citation on the doors of the church. Then the fellow put in an appearance and had a lawyer with him. He was planning to justify himself and he had others who sided with him. And the professors said that his champions must leave, for otherwise they were in violation of their oath[19] and going against the university ...

[After some negotiations which involved even the duke, whose support the professors invoked], the rector posted the decision on the church doors, that Aesticampianus was banned for ten years. There was much murmuring among the students. They said that the professors in council had done an injustice to Aesticampianus, but the professors themselves said they did not give a fig for that. And his boarders said that Aesticampianus was going to avenge this injustice and cite the university before the papal court in Rome, but the professors laughed and said: 'Hah! What can that vagabond do!' And you must know that there is now great concord at the university. And Professor Delitsch lectures on the humanities. And Professor Rotburg[20] likewise, who composed a book that is more than three times as great as all of Virgil's[21] works. And he put much into his book that is well said and in defence of the holy mother church, and in praise of the saints. And he commends our university and holy theology and the faculty of arts, and he reprehends those secular poets, those heathens. And our professors say that his verses are as good as the verses of Virgil and are flawless, for he knows the art of versifying perfectly, and was a good versifier even before he reached the age of twenty. For this reason the professors in council promised that he could lecture on his book rather than on Terence,[22] for it was more needed than Terence and had good Christian stuff in it, and does not deal with prostitutes and buffoons as does Terence. You must spread this news in your university. Then Buschius[23] will perhaps suffer the same fate as Aesticampianus.

When will you send me your book against Reuchlin? You say much about it, but nothing happens. You wrote that you will actually send it to me, and you don't do it. God forgive you: you don't like me as much as I like you, for you are to me as dear as my own heart. Still, send it along, for I very much desire to read this book and share the feast with you, so to speak. And tell me your news. And compose a saying or some verses about me, if I am worthy of it. So farewell in Christ our Lord and God, for ever and ever. Amen.

I.25 From Magister Philipp Sculptoris to Magister Ortwin Gratius

As I've often told you, I am very upset because that scum, I mean the faculty of poets, is growing and expanding in every province and region. In my time there was only one poet, called Samuel,[24] but now there are more than twenty poets in this town and they harass us because we side with the old ways. Just recently I ran into someone who said that *scholaris*[25] did not denote a person who went to school to learn. I said: 'You ass, do you want to correct the Holy Doctor[26] who uses that word?' He immediately went and wrote an invective against me in which he put much shameful stuff, and he said that I am not a good grammarian because I did not explain this word correctly when I lectured on the first part of Alexander[27] and on the book *De modis significandi*.[28] I want to write to you about those terms so that you can see that I interpret them correctly ... [The writer gives a number of fanciful etymologies.] This fellow declares that this is incorrect and embarrassed me before my students. I then said it was good enough for a man's eternal salvation to know simple grammar and know how to express his thoughts. Then he replied that I know neither simple nor double grammar, that I know nothing at all. Then I was pleased because now I can cite him for breach of the privileges of the University of Vienna, where he will have to answer me. I am a graduate, for God's sake, an MA. And if I proved learned enough for a whole university, I am learned enough for a single poet, for the university is more powerful than a poet. And believe me I wouldn't do without this injury, not if someone paid me twenty florins.[29]

They say here that all poets want to side with Doctor Reuchlin against the theologians, and that one of them already composed a book called 'The Triumph of Reuchlin,'[30] and that it contains many scandals about you. I wish all the poets were sent to the land where pepper grows and left us in peace. Now one must fear that the faculty of art will perish on account of those poets. They themselves say that the members of the faculty of arts lead the young people astray and take money off them and make them bachelors and magisters even if they are ignorant. And the result is that the students do not want to graduate in the arts. All want to be poets. I have a friend who is a good young man and has good brains, and his parents sent him to Ingolstadt, and I gave him letters of reference addressed to a certain magister who is well qualified in the arts and is about to graduate with a doctorate in theology. But that young man left the magister and went to the poet Philomusus[31] and listened to his lectures. I pity the young man, as is written in Proverbs 19[:17]: 'He pays the Lord, who pities the poor.' If he had stayed with the magister until now, he would be a Bachelor. But as it is, he is nothing, even if he studies poetry for ten years. I know that you too have a lot of trouble from these secular poets, even if you yourself are a poet, but not a poet of this kind. You are on the side of the church and are well grounded in theology. And when you put together poems, they are not about vanities but about praising the saints. I would gladly find out how matters stand with Doctor Reuchlin. If I can be of any use to you in this matter, let me know and inform me about everything at the same time. Farewell.

I.37 Lupold Federfusius, soon to be licentiate, to Magister Gratius

As many greetings as there are blades of grass eaten by the geese! Herr Magister Ortwin, a very subtle question has come up in the quodlibeticals[32] at Erfurt between the faculties of theology and natural philosophy: one party says, when a Jew becomes a Christian, his foreskin, the part of his member that is cut off at birth according to the Jewish law, grows back. This is the view of the theological faculty, who offer a number of magisterial proofs for it. One is that Jews who have converted to Christianity could still be regarded as Jews at the Last Judgment when their member is bared, and so they would suffer injustice. But the Lord is unjust to no man, therefore, etc. They draw another argument from the words of the psalmist, who says: 'He covers me in the day of trouble, he covers me in the secret place.'[33] The 'day of trouble' means the Day of Doom in the Valley of Josephat when an account of all sins must be rendered. I'll omit the other arguments for brevity's sake, because we at Erfurt are moderns, and the moderns like brevity, as you know. Also, my memory is bad, and I cannot learn by heart a great number of citations, as do the jurists.

There is another party, however, contending that this argument does not hold up, and they cite Plautus[34] in their support, who says in his poetry: 'What is done cannot be undone.' On this basis they prove that a Jew who, when he was a Jew, lost a portion of his body, will not recover it when he is of the Christian faith. They also argue that their opponents' proof does not have a formal logical conclusion, because it follows from the major premise that Christians, who have lost part of their member on account of their indecent lifestyle (and it has happened many times both to laymen and clerics), would be mistaken for Jews at the Last Judgment. But this is a heretical conclusion, and our professors, the inquisitors of heretical pravity, will not tolerate it, especially since they themselves are sometimes defective in that part – but not as a result of consorting with prostitutes but because they have been careless in the baths.

I beg Your Worship most humbly and devotedly to establish the truth of this matter once and for all by asking Herr Pfefferkorn's wife. You are on good terms with her, and she will not refuse to answer whatever you ask her in the name of your close friendship with her husband. I hear, moreover, that you are her father confessor and therefore can force her to obey on pain of punishment. Say to her: 'Don't be ashamed, Mistress. I know you are as respectable as any woman in Cologne. I am not asking you anything that is not honourable. Only tell me the truth: Does your husband have a foreskin or not? Speak up, don't be ashamed. By the love of God, why are you silent?' But I don't want to give you instructions. You know better than I how to deal with women. In haste from Erfurt: from the house of the Dragon.[35]

I.46 From Johann Currificis Ambachensis to Magister Ortwin Gratius

[The writer has transferred from the University of Cologne to another university. He writes to his former professor.]

Let me tell you about the poets. There is one here who lectures on Valerius Maximus,[36] but I don't enjoy it half as much as I enjoyed it when you lectured on Valerius Maximus at Cologne. All he does is expound the text itself, whereas when you came to the parts about religion being neglected, about dreams and auspices, you quoted holy scripture, that is, the *Catena Aurea* of St Thomas which is called the *Continuum*,[37] and Durandus[38] and other shining lights of theology and asked us to note down these passages, draw a hand in the margin,[39] and learn them by heart. You must know that not so many students are enrolled here as in Cologne, because at Cologne the students can be beggars (some of them even have to steal food), but here this is not allowed. Everyone must take his meals in residence and be properly registered in the university. But although there are few students, they are insolent, just as insolent as many are at Cologne. Recently, they 'staircased' a don at the residence. He was standing outside someone's room and listening to the partying inside, when someone came out and, finding him listening, threw him downstairs. They are so bold here that they fight with the patrol ... and go around with drawn swords and ropes and sabres and pieces of lead attached to a cord, which they can throw and draw back again. A little while ago the patrol struck a student on the head so that he fell to the ground, but he got up and socked them one and fought them off. There is still another thing: please ask Professor Arnold von Tungern, who is no trifling theologian, whether it is a sin to play dice for indulgences.[40] I know some fellows who are scoundrels who have gambled away all the indulgences given them by Jacob Hoogstraten, when he ended the lawsuit of Reuchlin in Mainz.[41] There were three fellows there, and they said that indulgences are of no value to people. If it is a sin [to gamble on indulgences], and I believe it is, and it could not possibly not be a sin, I know who the [gamblers] are and I want to denounce them to the Dominicans ...

II.46 From Magister Cunradus Unckebunck to Magister Ortwin Gratius

... I hear you have few pupils and complain that Buschius and Caesarius[42] lure students away from you – although they are not as skilled as you in expounding the poets allegorically and in citing scriptural passages as well. I think the devil is in those poets! They ruin the universities. I heard from a professor at Leipzig, who has been teaching for thirty-six years, and he told me that when he was young, the universities were well off because there was not a poet within twenty miles. He told me, too, that students diligently attended lectures, both at the university and in their residences. It was considered a great scandal that a student should walk in the street without having Peter of Spain or the *Parva Logicalia*[43] under his arm. And if they studied grammar, they had Alexander or the *Vade mecum* or the *Exercitium puerorum* or the *Opus minus*[44] or the sayings of Johannes Sinthen[45] with them. And in class they paid due attention, and they respected the professors in the arts faculty. And if they saw a professor they were as terrified as if they had seen the devil. He told me that in those days there were four graduations of bachelors each year, and on each occasion there were always fifty or sixty graduands. In those days the university was flourishing; and when a student had been in residence for a year and a half he was made BA, and after three years, or two and a half, MA. Therefore his parents were satisfied and gladly supplied money, since they saw that their sons were on the way to respectable positions. But today students feel they must attend lectures on Virgil and Pliny[46] and the rest of the newfangled authors. What is more, they may listen to them for five years and never get a degree. And so, when they return home, their parents ask them: 'So what are you now?' and they reply that they are nothing, that they have been studying poetry. And then the parents don't know what to think. They see that their sons have not graduated and they are dissatisfied with the university and sorry for the money they have spent. Then they say to others: 'Don't send your sons to university. They'll learn nothing and spend their nights in town, fooling around. And the money paid out for their studies is wasted.'

The same professor told me, furthermore, that in his time there were some 2000 students in Leipzig and the same number in Erfurt, and 4000 in Vienna and the same number in Cologne and in other cities. Now there aren't as many students in all the universities together as there were formerly in one or two. And the professors of Leipzig complain a great deal about the scarcity of students. The poets do great damage. And when the parents send their sons to the residences and colleges, they don't want to stay there, and go instead to the poets and study bad stuff. He said that he had forty boarders once in Leipzig, and when he went to church or to the market or for a walk, they walked behind him. And if anyone confessed in confession that he had secretly taken a course on Virgil from a Bachelor, the priest imposed a great penance on him, for example, fasting for sixty days or praying every day the seven penitential psalms. And he swore a holy oath to me that he saw one graduand rejected because one of the examiners had once seen him reading Terence on a feast day. I wish things were like that at universities today, for then I would not have to drudge here at the papal court. For what could I do at the university? One can't make a living there. The students don't want to stay in residences or be tutored by a professor. Of twenty students hardly one or two intend to proceed to graduation. All the others want to study the humanities. And if a professor gives a lecture, he has no audience because the poets have so many listeners in their tutorials that it is a miracle. All universities in Germany are affected. Therefore we must pray to God that all poets may die, for 'it is better that one perishes, etc.,' that is, that the poets of whom there are only a few in any one university may die rather than that so many universities perish. Write to me hereafter, or at least apologize for neglecting me. Farewell. Written from Rome.

II. 58 From Magister Irus Perlirus to Magister Ortwin Gratius

Copious greetings, venerable sir. We have received here at the university the writings you have composed against Johann Reuchlin. The old professors here give it high praise, but the new, young ones don't think much of them, saying that you harass the good Reuchlin out of envy. And at our last meeting when we debated what to do about the *Eye Mirror*, those new professors who have no experience opposed the old ones, saying that Reuchlin is innocent and never wrote anything heretical. And if they give us so much trouble, I don't know what will happen next. I believe that all the universities will perish on account of those poets. There are so many now that it is amazing. Recently someone arrived here, called Petrus Mosellanus,[47] and he is a teacher of Greek. There is also another who lectures on Greek, Richard Croke by name,[48] and he comes from England. And I recently said: 'The Devil! He comes from England?' I believe if they had a poet in the land where pepper grows, he would immediately come to Leipzig! That is the reason why the professors have a pitiful number of students. I remember that in days gone by when a professor went to the baths more pupils attended him than now go to church on a feast day. Moreover students then were as well behaved as angels. Now they run all over the place and pay no heed to professors. And they all want to live in town and to have their meals away from their residences, and the professors have very few boarders. On the last graduation day, only ten Bachelors graduated; and when we held the examination the professors talked about rejecting certain candidates. Then I said: 'No way! If we reject one of them, no one will come forward for examination henceforth, or even study for the degree – they will go to the poets.' And so we made allowances for them and let them pass. We found grounds for dispensation under three heads. First, concerning the candidate's age, for the rule is that one must be at least sixteen years old to obtain a BA, and twenty for an MA. But if they are not of full age, a dispensation may be granted.

Second, we have the power to give a dispensation concerning conduct. If undergraduates have failed to show sufficient respect to professors and graduates, they must be rejected – unless admitted by dispensation. And for this purpose there is an inquiry into misbehaviour: whether they have been uncivil in the streets, or have gone to prostitutes, or have borne arms, or have addressed a professor or a priest with 'thou,' or have made a disturbance during lectures or at their residence.

Third there is a dispensation with regard to skills, when candidates do not have enough knowledge in their dicipline and have not fulfilled the prerequisites. A little while ago, during an examination, I asked one candidate: 'Tell me, why don't you give an answer?' He replied it was because he was shy. 'Hardly!' I said. 'I think you are ignorant, not shy.' Then he said: 'By God, no, Herr Professor, I have great knowledge in my head, but it won't come out.' So I gave him a dispensation. You see that the universities are losing out. I have a boarder, whom I recently interrogated about misbehaviour. He immediately turned on me and addressed me with 'thou.' Then I said: 'I'll remember that when you graduate,' hinting that he might suffer rejection. He answered: 'Shit on you and your BA! I'll go to Italy where teachers do not cheat their pupils and have no such fantastical nonsense when they grant the degree of bachelor. If a man is learned, the degree is conferred on him; if he is not, he is treated like any other ass.' Then I said: 'You rascal! Do you belittle the degree of BA, which is a great honour?' He replied that he did not care even for the MA. And he said: 'I have heard from a friend that when he lived in Bologna he saw that all the MAs from Germany were inducted like freshmen; not so the undergraduates. For in Italy it is considered a disgrace to hold a BA or MA from a German University.'

You see what scandals there are. I wish all the universities would join together and put an end to all those poets and humanists who ruin the universities ... Farewell. Written in Leipzig.

## II.59 From Johann Coclearlignius to Magister Ortwin Gratius

You commissioned me to inquire of the merchants coming here from all regions during the fair about that plot about which you have had letters, that is, the conspiracy of certain poets and jurists who want to defend Johann Reuchlin and write against the theologians of Cologne, and against the Dominicans, unless they immediately leave the aforesaid Johann Reuchlin in peace. Let me tell you that I inquired diligently and finally came across a bookseller from the southern region. He told me some amazing things. He named some of the conspirators and said that he had seen the writings they exchange. He said that Doctor Murner[49] was practically the head of the conspiracy, and he knew very well that he was the author of a book about the evil deeds of the Dominicans and another defending Reuchlin. He also mentioned Hermann Buschius.[50] He said he had seen a letter from him in which he promises his fellow conspirators that he will not be the last one among them but boldly stand up on behalf of Reuchlin. Then he said the Count of Neuenahr,[51] canon of Cologne, was another member of the conspiracy and he had composed some amazing stuff about the theologians, which he wanted to publish immediately. Then there is a certain Willibald,[52] who I think lives in Nürnberg. He has uttered many threats and said that he will drive away all the theologians with his writings ... then he named a certain Eobanus Hessus[53] of Erfurt, a young man, it seems, and a very skilful poet and he has a friend, Petreius Aperbach by name.[54] And the two are now writing certain books that they will immediately publish unless the theologians make peace with Reuchlin. Then there is an Englishman at Leipzig, I don't know his name, but I believe he is the one who was for two years in Cologne.[55] He too is one of them. In addition, there is Vadianus[56] in Vienna, who is said to be a terrific poet. And a certain Caspar Ursinus[57] at the court of the cardinal, ... he wants to be among the conspirators, too. The bookseller furthermore named Philip Melanchthon, Jacob Wimpheling, Beatus Rhenanus, and Nicolaus Gerbellius,[58] all conspirators. He said that they write letters to Ulrich Hutten, a student in Bologna, who must also be one of them. The merchant knew of no others. Then I asked others whether Erasmus of Rotterdam took part in the conspiracy. And a certain merchant said: 'Erasmus is a man for himself, but certainly he will never be a friend of those theologians and friars. And he has clearly defended Johann Reuchlin[59] in his conversations and in his writings and has written to the pope on his behalf.'

Others told me that Paulus Riccius[60] belongs to the group as well. Some say that Johannes Cuspinianus and Konrad Peutinger,[61] who enjoys the favour of the emperor, also are in contact with this group and do all in their power to thwart the theologians of Cologne and to honour Johann Reuchlin. A student at Erfurt who is a friend of mine says that Konrad Mutianus[62] is the worst among the Reuchlinists, and that he hates the theologians so much that he cannot even bear hearing the theologians of Cologne mentioned. He says he has seen some twenty letters of Mutianus in which he urges some friends to support Reuchlin. This is all I have heard up to now. If I learn more, I will write to you. Farewell in Christ. From Frankfurt.

**Notes**

1 *Praedicamenta*, 7.1; similarly *Metaphysica*, 2.1. Aristotle was the main authority in the scholastic system. Scholars were expected to be able to quote his writings on logic.
2 From the twelfth century on, the church differentiated between venial and mortal sins. Classification was not always easy. Humanists regarded the preoccupation of professional theologians with definitions, divisions, and categorizations as quibbles.
3 Parish priests could not grant absolution from certain sins; they were 'reserved,' i.e., the sinner could be absolved only by someone in the higher echelons of the church hierarchy, such as the local bishop or the pope, or their legal representatives.
4 Jews were required by law to wear distinctive clothing. See above, p. 5. An actual incident similar to the one described in the fictitious letter here is related by John Evelyn in 1645: 'The Jewes in Rome wore red hatts till the Cardinal of Lions, being short-sighted, lately saluted one of them, thinking him to be a cardinal, as he passed by his coach; on which an order was made that they should use only the yellow colour' (quoted in *On the Eve of the Reformation*, ed. H. Holborn, 252 n. 11).
5 Ulrich von Hutten. It is likely that an actual incident is described here.
6 On Meyer, see above, p. 107 n. 8.
7 A standard textbook by Peter Lombard, bishop of Paris (d. 1160), containing a collection of doctrinal opinions drawn from patristic writings.
8 Verulanus Sulpitius taught at Rome in the fifteenth century. His work on metric composition was a popular textbook.
9 Jerome, *Epistle*, XCVII.11.
10 It was customary to accept cheese from peasants in lieu of alms.
11 A reference to John 8:48.
12 On Tungern, see above, p. 108 n. 20.
13 Johannes Aesticampianus (1460–1520) lectured on classical authors at the University of Leipzig, 1507–10. He was ousted and moved to the University of Wittenberg, where he taught until his death.
14 Pliny (c. 23–79 AD) is the author of a handbook of natural history. He wrote in prose. Here and elsewhere 'poet' is used as a term of reproach to denote humanists.
15 One of the standard textbooks of logic in the scholastic curriculum. The author, Peter of Spain (d. 1277), was elected Pope John XXI in 1276.
16 The two main theological schools, following the teachings of Thomas Aquinas ('Thomists') and Duns Scotus ('Scotists') respectively.

17 Thomas Aquinas; see below, n. 26.
18 Andreas Delit(z)sch taught at Leipzig. In 1513 he lectured on the Roman poet Ovid's *Metamorphoses* in the faculty of arts, that is, in the undergraduate part of the university.
19 Graduands had to swear an oath of loyalty to their university, i.e., that they would 'defend the status, statutes, and privileges [of the university and its professors] all your lifetime, to whatever position you may come' (L. Thorndike, *University Records and Life in the Middle Ages* [New York, 1944], 104).
20 Johannes Tyberinus of Rotenburg ob der Tauber, the author of a book of poems, *Musithias de caelitibus et sacris historiis* (Poems about Saints and Sacred History), Leipzig, 1514.
21 Virgil (70–19 BC), author of the epic *Aeneid*, is commonly regarded as the principal Roman poet.
22 Terence (c. 185–159 BC), Roman comic playwright.
23 For Buschius, see above, headnote.
24 Tentatively identified by Böcking as Samuel Haroch de Monte Rutilo, whose poems appear in fifteenth-century manuscripts from the Gotha region (Böcking, *Supplementum*. II: 463).
25 *scholaris* is an adjective, i.e., 'student-,' but it was commonly used as a noun, 'student.'
26 Thomas Aquinas (c. 1225–75), the most influential medieval theologian. His usage was not regarded as normative by humanists, who respected only classical usage.
27 Alexander de Villa Dei (fl. 1200), author of the *Doctrinale*, a popular Latin grammar.
28 A number of medieval authors had written grammatical treatises under this title. They are collectively known as 'Modistae.'
29 He is extremely pleased to have been insulted because he will now be able to sue the man for breach of his oath of loyalty. See above, n. 19.
30 Composed by Hutten in 1517, text in Böcking, *Supplementum*, III: 416–47.
31 Jacob Locher (1470–1528), called Philomusus (Lover of the Muses) taught at the University of Ingolstadt, where he became entangled in 1505 in a controversy with the theologians over the respective merits of theology and poetry.
32 Disputations were divided into ordinary disputations, which were part of the course and dealt with the principal doctrinal questions, and quodlibeticals (quodlibet = 'as you please') about minor questions that seemed specious and ludicrous to humanists.
33 Ps. 27:5.

34 *Amphitryo*, III.2, 3.
35 A student residence.
36 First century AD Roman historian, author of *Facta et dicta memorabilia* (Memorable Facts and Sayings).
37 A biblical commentary by Thomas Aquinas.
38 Durandus of St Pourcain (c. 1275–1334), scholastic philosopher.
39 The customary manner of marking a passage (the equivalent of using a marker to highlight a passage).
40 The sale of indulgences (papers that guaranteed the remission of time souls spent in purgatory) was used to finance papal building projects or campaigns against the Turks. The practice was attacked by Luther in the *Ninety-five Theses* (1517) and became an issue in the Reformation debate.
41 This is where the case was originally to be heard, but in November 1513 it was moved to Speyer at Reuchlin's request.
42 Johannes Caesarius (c. 1468–1550), studied at Cologne and Paris. He taught Greek in Cologne and Münster, and then went to Italy where he obtained a doctorate in medicine (Siena, 1513). On his return to Germany he tutored the sons of noblemen and edited classical texts.
43 See above, n. 15.
44 Alexander de Villa Dei (see above, n. 27); the textbooks mentioned are not extant.
45 Jan Sinthen (d. c. 1498) taught at a boys' school in Deventer and was the author of a number of grammatical works.
46 See above, nn. 14 and 21.
47 Petrus Mosellanus (d. 1524) taught Greek at the University of Leipzig; he was Croke's successor (see next note).
48 Richard Croke (d. 1530) taught Greek at the University of Leipzig from 1515 to 1517, when he returned to his native England to teach at Cambridge.
49 Thomas Murner (1475–1537), Franciscan, who acquired a doctorate in theology from the University of Freiburg and a doctorate in canon law from the University of Basel; he had some humanistic learning and supported Reuchlin. In the twenties he became a bitter opponent of Luther against whom he wrote a satire in German, *Der grosse Lutherische Narr* (The Great Lutheran Fool).
50 On Buschius, see above, headnote.
51 Count Hermann of Neuenahr (c. 1492–1530), studied under Caesarius in Cologne (see above, n. 42) and travelled with him to Italy; on his return he became archdeacon of the Cologne chapter and chancellor of the University of Cologne. He had many humanistic contacts and supported Reuchlin. See also below, Document 11, headnote.

52 Willibald Pirckheimer; see below, headnote to Document 8.
53 Eobanus Hessus (1488–1540), well-known poet, lectured on classical authors at the University of Erfurt. He was a supporter of Luther, and toward the end of his life accepted a position at the reformed University of Marburg.
54 Petreius Aperbach belonged to the humanistic circle at Erfurt and was a supporter of Reuchlin. Two of his letters to Reuchlin are extant.
55 I.e., Richard Croke. See above, n. 48.
56 Joachim Vadianus (1484–1551) taught Pliny and other classical authors at the University of Vienna; he acquired a doctorate in medicine (1517) and became town physician in his native St Gallen in Switzerland. He admired Luther and was instrumental in introducing the reformation in St Gallen.
57 Caspar Ursinus (d. 1539), Silesian humanist in the service of Cardinal Matthaeus Lang, taught Greek at the University of Vienna and later was appointed royal historian to King Ferdinand I of Austria.
58 The famous humanist and reformer Philip Melanchthon (1497–1560) began his teaching career in Tübingen and, in 1518, was appointed to the newly created chair of Greek at the University of Wittenberg.

Jacob Wimpheling (1450–1528) taught in the faculty of arts in Heidelberg; in 1496 he obtained a licence in theology, but continued to teach poetry and rhetoric. He remained loyal to the Catholic church and retired to a monastery in 1501.

Beatus Rhenanus (1485–1547), a historian and philologist, belonged to the humanistic circle in Basel. He left when the city turned Protestant in 1529 and returned to his native Selestat, continuing to devote himself to historical scholarship.

Nicolaus Gerbel (c. 1485–1560) held an MA from the University of Cologne and a doctorate in canon law from the University of Bologna; he was a jurist in the service of the Strasbourg cathedral chapter and active in literary circles there. In the twenties he became an ardent supporter of Luther.

59 See below, Document 9.
60 Paulus Riccius (d. 1541), a converted Jew, physician to Emperor Maximilian I, scholar of the cabala. He published an oration in defence of Reuchlin (*Apologetica oratio*, Nürnberg, 1523).
61 Johannes Cuspinianus (1473–1529), rector of the University of Vienna in 1500 and imperial councillor, was the leading light of the Viennese humanistic circle.

Konrad Peutinger (1470–1526), erudite jurist in the service of the Augsburg city council, was in frequent contact with Hutten and

Pirckheimer. He engaged in antiquarian studies and published a volume of Roman inscriptions.

62 Konrad Mutianus (1470–1526), a graduate of the universities of Erfurt and Ferrara (doctorate in canon law) became a canon in Gotha. He was a champion of humanistic studies and at the centre of the humanistic circle at Erfurt.

DOCUMENT 6

# Reports on the Confiscation of Jewish Books in Frankfurt, 1509

The following reports, written in Hebrew, come from a manuscript now in the city library in Amsterdam and published by I. Kracauer in 'Actenstücke zur Geschichte der Confiscation der hebräischen Schriften in Frankfurt a. M.,' *Monatsschrift für Geschichte der Wissenschaft des Judentums* 44 (1900), 119–21, 124–6. According to Kracauer they were copied from documents in the archive of the Jewish community in Frankfurt. They describe Pfefferkorn's actions, the resistance of the community to the confiscation of Jewish books, and their appeal to the emperor.

## 1. A Report on Pefferkorn's Actions

On Friday [28 September 1509] the butcher[1] came to us here in Frankfurt, together with three priests and two friends from the city council, and they seized the books in the synagogue – the Tefillot, Machzorim, and Selichot[2] – everything they could find, and forbade us in the name of the emperor to continue praying in the synagogue. It was [Pfefferkorn's] intention to return the following day and take also the books we have in our homes, for there was not enough time that day for him to complete the task. But the priests did not want to disturb the Sabbath, nor their own holiday, that is, the Sunday, which was the next day. On that same Friday we sent R. Jonathan to Worms to approach the justice department [Kammergericht] and see whether it might be possible to prevent this evil and to retain at least the books that are in our homes. But he was unable to accomplish anything. On Saturday, however, we sent R. Gumprecht Weissenan to the archbishop of Mainz in Aschaffenburg,[3] to ask him to command the priests to desist from this undertaking. He was successful with his request and, praise be to God, obtained help and salvation for the Jews. On Monday the Jew came with the priests and his friends, the councillors, to confiscate the books, and at that time R. Gumprecht had not yet returned. We therefore spent the day once more strenuously objecting to his initiative and indicating that we would appeal to the emperor. The priests and Pfefferkorn's friends, the councillors, then decided to bring the matter before the council on Tuesday, that they might examine and decide on the question of whether we had a right to appeal to the emperor after a direct order had been issued to us. The verdict of the city council ran: 'We should obey the mandate, and then appeal.' At the same time they decided to come in the afternoon [to continue with the confiscation]. Thank God, the letters of the archbishop of Mainz to the priests had arrived in the meantime. They instructed the priests to desist from this initiative and indicated that he would punish them for what they had done already. Once the priests had withdrawn, the council no longer had a right to do anything in this matter.[4] And on Wednesday [3 October], we sent R. Jonathan on horseback to the emperor, to frustrate the plans of the evil man [Pfefferkorn], and God gave success to his ways and his intentions. At the same time we sent L. Kneblen through all of Germany, into all regions, requesting [delegates] to come to us on [29 October], to deliberate and decide what to do. See the following letter.

[The letter addressed to the Jewish communities relates the experiences described above and invites delegates to meet in Frankfurt to decide on further action and the means of financing it. It concludes: 'Should any community ... refuse to send money and participate in our efforts ... they will not longer be regarded as members of the Association of the Remainder of Israel.' As a result of these deliberations, the Association sent Jonathan Levi Zion to the imperial court to negotiate a withdrawal of the mandate given to Pfefferkorn.]

## 2. Jonathan Levi Zion's Reports to the Frankfurt Community

Dear friends in the Frankfurt community, greetings to each of you personally. Why should I go on at length where there is no need? I wish to inform you that Hishkiah Levi and I, your servant, reached Bozen on [15 October 1509] and were detained here because of a lack of money. With much difficulty and at a high price we obtained a small horse and set out for Verona, for the emperor is said to be there or in the neighbourhood. Of course we shall now appear before him empty-handed, and it is to be feared, indeed practically certain, that I shall not be able to achieve anything until you send a man who is prepared for three things – you know what I mean.[5] Dear brothers, you are wise and reasonable men and consider everything, but I must admonish you, not to say, warn you: Listen and observe that, according to general opinion, it is now practically impossible to present or obtain a letter of credit in northern Italy, for the situation is unfortunately still uncertain, even after the emperor and his military machine have withdrawn from Padua.[6] Indeed, the tensions are rising every day, and as might be expected, it is quite obscure and unfathomable how this is going to end. Therefore, dear brothers, consider that you obliged me to travel in this business against my will. Do not desert me and supply me with money as soon as possible so that I shall not be forced to borrow money here at 100 per cent. You need not be afraid or anxious, for I shall be close-fisted whenever possible. I will be lavish only if I am forced to spend money to avoid suffering embarrassment (which God forbid!) …

[He reports again on 15 November 1509]

Dear friends! In the end the margrave of Baden[7] sent a message to the Jewish council house at Verona on [26 October 1509], asking the Jews to come to his quarters and inform him of the contents of the request concerning the apostate [Pfefferkorn], for our lord, the emperor, had appointed him [the margrave] our legal representative [procurator]. Thus I went to him on Friday and was with him for some three hours: he, his chancellor, and I. He had an appeal made out, as you can see from the copy. For this I gave him something, and should we obtain what we are asking for in the petition, I shall give him an additional one hundred Gulden for his efforts. And so he acted on our behalf and made a great personal effort … but what shall I say? Everything is upside down. The apostate and his courtiers have persuaded the emperor to write to the archbishop that [Pfefferkorn] should be the commissioner in this business, together with the apostate Viktor [von Karben] in Cologne, another doctor from Cologne,[8] a doctor from Heidelberg, and Doctor Reuchlin from Stuttgart. In referring to the commission, the emperor emphasized that the archbishop of Mainz had interfered with the apostate and kept him from confiscating all books. He asked the archbishop to support Pfefferkorn and the doctors when they came together, and to have all our books read and carefully examined according to the original mandate ... We protested against this commission and sent a second appeal to the emperor, as you can see from the enclosed copy. But it is very likely that the apostate will be commissioned to proceed. For on [14 November] in the evening, Isaac of Triest told me that he had made careful enquiries and had discovered that the council of the city of Frankfurt made out a report about us and gave it to the apostate. It said that we resisted the imperial mandate and that we did so declaring that 'the emperor had no jurisdiction over us; it was up to the council to command us.' The emperor and his councillors were most irate about this, so that it is to be feared that they [the council] deliberately set out to bring great evil upon us. You must immediately send wise and prudent men from our communities to the emperor. They must of course be well supplied with gold and silver, and must beseech the emperor to be merciful and spare us. Perhaps the All Merciful will take pity on us and look upon us with favourable eyes. For I fear things that I do not want to write down. If the marshall of the archbishop had not loaned me money, I could not have paid for my expenses here. I have told you nothing but the truth. Consider it well and act according to your best counsel. May God have pity on us.

**Notes**

1 Pfefferkorn denied that he had been a butcher. See above, p. 3.
2 The standard prayer book, the prayerbook for feast days, and special prayers (usually for Yom Kippur).
3 Uriel of Gemmingen; see above, p. 96, n. 20.
4 The confiscation was a matter of ecclesiastical jurisdiction in which the council was merely the executive arm.
5 He is presumably alluding to Gen 32:8, where Jacob prepares to appease Esau with gifts. Rashi's commentary on the passage refers to three methods of defence against an enemy: prayers, bribes to win the enemy's good will, and as a final measure, combat.
6 From 1495 until his death in 1516, Maximilian was embroiled in wars in Italy. His aim was to prevent the French from taking control of Milan. Italian cities, in turn, engaged in a diplomatic dance, trying to use the emperor to rid themselves of the French invaders.
7 Christoph I (1475–1527), who had been delegated by the emperor to look into the business of the Jewish books.
8 Probably, Hoogstraten is meant.

DOCUMENT 7

# Two Reports by the Faculty of Theology at Cologne

## 1. The Report on the Question of the Jewish Books

On the request of the Emperor, the Archbishop of Mainz obtained reports on Pfefferkorn's proposal from a number of sources, among them the faculty of theology at Cologne. The theologians submitted the following report in November 1510 (Latin text in Böcking *Supplementum*, 1:94–5).

... Because the Jewish book called Talmud manifestly contains not only errors and false statements, but also blasphemies and heresies against their own law ... [Popes] Gregory and Innocent ordered the said book to be burned.[1] The Jews may have many other books that are impious and contain horrible blasphemies (as is said) against our Lord Jesus Christ and the Christians, his faithful followers. Once this is established, it would be impious and irreligious to allow them the use of such books which they, who are mockers and blasphemers of the Lord Christ, might use to teach their children. From this it may be suspected that the rest of their books are corrupt as well and do not convey the intention of Moses' books and those of other prophets and wise men. Taking these and other matters (omitted for brevity's sake) into consideration, we consider it advisable, praiseworthy, godly, salutary, reasonable, and in the interest of the Christian faith as well as of the Jews' salvation that all these and other books (excepting the whole Old Testament, which they are permitted to use) be taken away with Christian restraint and piety and be set aside with a public and official declaration that this is done solely to distinguish between books which the Jews are permitted to have for the true understanding of the Old Law and those which they are not permitted to have or read. Once this has been decided, the books that are legitimate ought to be returned to them; the illegitimate ones ought to be destroyed or set aside. When all the passages that appear to be suspect are collected out of all their books by men who know the Jewish language, let the Jews be called publicly and let their arguments concerning these passages be listened to in full and examined. And if they acknowledge that these passages contain errors, they will understand that such books are not useful to them. If, however, they remain obstinately opposed to the truth, the prince[2] will have to decide whether they are morally wrong or create and follow heresies that go against their law. And to remove any cause of complaint, if it is decided to burn the books and if there is no good reason why the Christians should reserve them, the law about burning the Talmud could be renewed ... Furthermore, it seems expedient to prevent the Jews from practising usury and to allow them to take up honest work for a living, but let them be distinguished from Christians by a badge, and let them be taught in their own language by experienced converts about the true law and the prophets for the glory of God, their own salvation, and the increase of the Christian religion, with the help of our Lord God and with your [the archbishop's] and the emperor's zealous cooperation.

### 2. On Reuchlin's *Eye Mirror*

After Reuchlin published his report in the *Eye Mirror*, the faculty examined the book for theological errors. Reuchlin's first reaction was to placate the theologians and adopt a humble attitude (see above, p. 18). Their first official response to him was therefore polite. The Latin text of the following missive, dated January 1512, and entitled 'A Christian instruction from the University of Cologne to Johann Reuchlin for the purpose of doing away and suppressing his error,' is printed in Böcking, *Supplementum*, I: 125–7.

Respected and excellent sir: At the last Frankfurt Fair a tract entitled *Eye Mirror* published under your name was brought to our attention. We had it examined by some of our faculty members and found it contained things we had never expected from you or any good Christian. In this tract you make every effort to advise the Reverend Father in Christ and elector, Our Gracious Lord Uriel, archbishop of Mainz, and through him the Most Serene Imperial Majesty, concerning the business of the Jewish books, trying to persuade them to reverse the praiseworthy initiative taken by the said Royal Majesty. To do this more effectively, as you perhaps thought, you wrote much that was of no relevance whatsoever, as if you had wanted to take up anything that occurred to your mind and gather it together. In doing so and hastening to achieve your end, you have been careless and have failed to note whether you were gathering an ill assortment of roses, stinging nettles, or evil-smelling flowers. In this manner you appeared before Christian readers as a champion of the perfidious Jews. And you made this impression also on the Jews themselves, who are hostile toward the cross and the blood through which we have been purified and redeemed. As we hear, they read your tract, which has been written and published in our vernacular language, and disseminated it. Thus you have given them an opportunity to deride us more than ever, for they found that among Christians and especially Christians who had a reputation for great learning, you were the only one who spoke on their behalf and maintained and defended their cause ...

To persuade His Imperial Majesty you have here and there inserted propositions that do not sound right and are offensive to the pious ears of faithful Christians and have rendered yourself suspect of thinking thoughts about our religion, our sacred scripture and its ecclesiastic exegetes, thoughts that are not as chaste or pure or sincere as they ought to be. About this we are more distraught than we can tell you ... but in the past days Professors Arnold of Tungern and Konrad Kolin,[3] our fellow faculty members, have shown and read to us letters you sent them, by which we were much comforted, for in them you admit your weakness and your unintentional mistake humbly and in a Catholic manner, asking them to commend you to our assembly and in which you explain specific points and give them a more positive meaning. This they have done with great charity and diligently, as you requested. By means of these letters they have persuaded us to regard you as a true and obedient and truly catholic son of the church, and we will continue to regard you as such if you attempt to take back the evil seed you have sown and to remove the stones which have been a stumbling block to others in the road of God ... [We enclose our censures] and ask that you give us a more detailed account of your position on these points in writing or, after the example of the humble and wise Augustine, recant and retract them.[4] For this is genuine and truly Christian severity tempered with charity, to correct and emend a work which contains unintentional and poorly considered hasty remarks, in so far as unsullied faith reigns with integrity in you.

**Notes**

1 Pope Gregroy IX forbade the Talmud in 1239, after being petitioned by the Jewish convert Nicholas Donin. The prohibition was renewed by Innocent IV in 1244. He described the Talmud as a book 'in which are manifest blasphemies against God and Christ and the blessed Virgin, intricate fables, erroneous abuses, and unheard-of stupidities.' If the Jews were deprived of this book, they would recognize the truth and 'be converted to the faith and humbly return to their Redeemer.' It was time to reinforce Pope Gregory's injunctions and proceed with severity. He ordered 'the aforesaid abusive books condemned ... and burned by fire wherever they can be found' and demanded that the Jews acknowledge that they were 'condemned by the Lord, whose death they wickedly plotted, and [should] at least outwardly recognize themselves as servants of those whom the death of Christ has made free and themselves slaves' (L. Thorndike, *University Records and Life in the Middle Ages* [New York, 1944], 48–9).

2 Presumably the Prince-Bishop Uriel of Gemmingen is meant.

3 For Tungern see above, p. 108, n. 20; the Dominican Konrad Kolin (or Köllin) was a member of the Cologne faculty of theology. See Peterse, *Jacobus Hoogstraeten*, 30–1.

4 The Church Father St Augustine (342–430 AD) acknowledged his mistakes in a book, entitled *Retractations*.

DOCUMENT 8

# Willibald Pirckheimer's Defence of Reuchlin, 1517

Willibald Pirckheimer (1470–1530) was a jurist by profession. He studied in Italy (Padua, Pavia), but returned in 1495 to serve on the council of his native city, Nürnberg. He remained a member of the council until his resignation in 1523. In 1499 he led imperial troops against the Swiss and was subsequently appointed imperial councillor by Charles V. He was a polymath and well-known champion of humanistic studies, publishing a number of editions and translations of classical authors. He sympathized with the Reformation in the beginning and was designated a Lutheran in the papal bull condemning Luther. This involved him in drawn-out negotiations with the papal court, which finally accepted his recantation. When Nürnberg turned Protestant in 1525, Pirckheimer found himself isolated. He had by this time become disillusioned with the reformers, whom he now depicted as troublemakers. The efforts of the city council to abolish monastic institutions affected him personally because a number of his sisters and daughters had taken religious vows.

Pirckheimer took an active interest in the Reuchlin affair and published a defence of the scholar. It appeared, together with a Latin edition of the Greek satirist Lucian's dialogue *Piscator* (Fisherman), in Nürnberg, 1517. My translation is based on the Latin text in *Willibald Pirckheimers Briefwechsel*, ed. D. Wuttke and H. Scheible (Munich, 1989), vol. 3, # 464, pp. 150–64.

They call me a Reuchlinist. Far from regretting this epithet, I am very glad of it. I would even say that nothing among the external goods that a merciful God has indulgently bestowed on me pleases me more than the friendship of good men, especially friendship that has not come about by chance but through literary fellowship. I value it so highly that I do not hesitate to equate it with the honours bestowed by the most powerful princes. Therefore I rejoice in and am proud of the wealth of learned friends I have, not only in Germany but in practically all of Europe. That great Erasmus of Rotterdam is one of my friends,[1] that model of nature's perfection, whom they do not scruple to call an eloquent theologian in their slanderous pamphlet, as if he had no other accomplishments except eloquence. The celebrated and most learned Reuchlin is my friend as well. They are men who not only excel in leading a blameless life but also abound in intellectual accomplishments, are conspicuous for their knowledge of various languages, are felicitious in expression as well as in all-round learning, excel in the most select disciplines and most varied knowledge – in short, like heroes they have won a truly splendid victory in the game of fortune and their glorious virtue almost surpasses human nature. Whatever they want to call me – Erasmian or Reuchlinist – they should realize that I do not consider them terms of reproach but rather of praise.

I would not be free of blame, however, if I did not defend my old friend Reuchlin, especially if I did not defend him against the most insolent attacks of invidious men and the impudent, no, criminal, lies they have invented. And yet some of them are laughable and others should be treated with contempt like old wives' tales. One charge, however, which they bring against that excellent man in their slanderous pamphlets must not be allowed to pass, in my opinion. For they are saying that he extorted gold from the Jews and was not ashamed to write many perverted things to do them a favour ... What would have impelled such a Christian man to commit so great a crime, deigning to prefer the friendship of the Jews to faith and truth? Love for the Jews? Then he would indeed deserve to be hated. Wrath against Christian piety and contempt for the true religion? But this is so unbelievable that no one in his right mind would invent it or dare to believe it. Nor could he have been motivated by other passions, for he is quite a stranger to them. What could have motivated him then to prefer the friendship of the Jews to the truth? They rightly ask what advantage, what wealth might have served as inducements that he should be so blinded by cupidity. After all, he is a man of advanced years, who has already enjoyed positions of honour, who was born from Christian parents – why then would he venture on such a shameful deed? He did not labour under poverty but was well-to-do, he has no sons to whom he could leave any ill-gotten gains, he needed little more in view of his age, and he knew beyond all doubt, even if he was ready to succumb to detestable avarice, that the Jews in their innate avarice would not part with a great deal of money, and a little would do him no good ...

[Reuchlin's enemies, the theologians of Cologne, pretend that they are the defenders of the faith, that they are acting out of zeal for the faith, but they are disgracing their profession.] I wish these grave men had acted more modestly and with more respect. As it is, they have besmirched the great name of theology with their clever lies and have dared to profane the majesty of philosophy. Even if they regard their adversaries as worthy of abuse, holy theology is above abuse. It is unworthy of the Christian faith to be defended by a neophyte,[2] to be carried on his shoulders like the world. The faith that brings salvation surely is not so lacking in people that the mysteries of our faith must be committed to a stranger, not to say, that the sheep must be committed to the wolf.

But, they say, [Pfefferkorn] has gained many souls for God. Indeed, if they are like him, and begin to prowl among the faithful like evil spirits and wicked demons, it shall become clear whether it can be called a gain or rather a loss that he has sown the seeds of such bitter discord and raised such a tumult among Christians. Spain will serve as a warning to us not to trust in extemporized and feigned conversions. It would have been much better for the so-called marranos to stay with their native perfidy than to simulate true religion and be Judaizers in secret. For we had several examples of what we can expect from these inveterate sinners who have been badly converted.[3] The emperor himself recently told a surprising and entertaining anecdote when he was in a large crowd in Augsburg. He wanted to indicate that converted Jews have as much in common with pious Christians as mice with cats.

Someone might object: if you detest abuse so much, do you think the abusive words of Reuchlin and the Reuchlinists are praiseworthy? Indeed, you yourself have called our respected helper a 'semi-Jew' and have expressed the cruel opinion that he should be erased from the world of the living (even though he is a Christian!). At the risk of condemning myself, I reply: I never liked abuse or the writers of abuse, especially those who, I knew, had not been attacked but had taken the initiative themselves and first hurled obscene jokes. But who would expect a sweeter or more pleasant sound from that ill-sounding and stinking bell,[4] not to speak of other nonsense that those admirable Reuchlin-flayers are writing, convinced that it is all decent and holy, being miserably deceived by no one but by themselves? Let them recognize, then, that it is their own fault and that they got what they deserved if their wonderful bell produced a lasting echo, a response worthy of it ...

[Pirckheimer emphasizes that his attack is not directed against theologians. The men who attack Reuchlin are not true theologians. To claim this title, a man must have the following qualifications, in Pirckheimer's opinion.] A theologian acquires this illustrious title, the title of great wisdom, not because he has a reputation [for being a great theologian] among the common people, not because his colleagues vainly flatter him, but as a result of sleepless nights, effort, pain, fasting, and immense and infinite labour. For in addition to grammar, he must know Latin, Greek, and Hebrew: Latin, because otherwise he will appear to be a barbarian rather than a theologian on account of his unpolished speech; Greek, because without it he can understand neither the encyclopedia of disciplines nor Aristotle himself, not to speak of its value for our faith; and Hebrew, because all the mysteries of the Old and New Testament are hidden in it. Next, he must also study dialectic, but genuine dialectic that stays within its prescribed limits. Furthermore, if a theologian knows nothing about rhetoric, I do not see how he can communicate the word of the Truth to the Christian people, if at any rate he intends to teach in a way that is intelligible to the people and if he wants to engage them emotionally, so that his message sticks in people's minds like the tip of an arrow. But if he wants to show off his learning and produces conclusions, corollaries, syllogisms, and the rest of the dialectical terms of which the common people are ignorant, they will of course go to sleep and his performance will leave them cold ...

[Returning to the Reuchlin Affair, Pirckheimer encourages the humanist to persevere in his studies.] Thus, most noble Reuchlin, do not yield to these misfortunes, but on the contrary go forward more boldly. For God has judged you worthy of trying the limits of your patience. It would have been no advantage to be praised by men whose approbation is wrong. 'If I pleased men,' the apostle says, 'I should not be the servant of Christ.'[5] There is no greater praise than unfair blame. It is written that a man will patiently bear misfortune for a time, and thereafter he will be rewarded and there will be rejoicing.[6] Your excellence is such that it lacks nothing, that nothing further could be added. You have served in positions of great distinction, you have lived a life that every good man would seek in his prayers, nature has united in you all its forces, you excel, you brim with erudition, you have been an ornament to Latin studies, you were the first to introduce Greek letters to Germany, you have studied Hebrew with a most admirable and singular dedication, you have left us numerous and by no means common demonstrations of your most felicitous intellect. You have mastered so many and unbelievably difficult skills that only one thing was lacking: to prove the greatness of your mind in some great adversity, just as gold is proved by fire. Behold, an excellent opportunity is afforded you, in which you may give us a unique specimen of your constant and upright character. Embrace this opportunity with good cheer and sustain adversity with equanimity and patience, [and avoid] violent language and audacious words, which are the signs and proof of criminal minds. Any innocent person can be slanderously accused, but only the guilty can be convicted; and 'it is ill fortune that discovers a great exemplar.'[7] God chastises whom he loves, and scourges everyone whom he receives as his son.[8] If you do not enter the competition, you cannot carry off the crown.[9] For has any saint ever obtained his crown without tribulation? And has any man ever been so fortunate (if human affairs can be fortunate) as to live a life without misery, calamity, or at any rate, adversity?

**Notes**

1 See headnote to Document 9.
2 I.e, Pfefferkorn.
3 Jews had been expelled from Spain in 1492. Those who converted to Christianity (called 'marranos') were suspected of practising their old religion in secret. These 'relapsed' Jews constituted one of the largest groups prosecuted by the Spanish Inquisition at the beginning of the sixteenth century.
4 A reference to a pamphlet recently published by Pfefferkorn, entitled *Sturmglock* (Warning Bell).
5 Gal. 1:10.
6 Sir. 1:29.
7 Seneca, *De providentia*, 3.4.
8 Heb. 12:6.
9 2 Tim. 2:5.

## DOCUMENT 9

# Two Letters from Erasmus Concerning the Reuchlin Affair

Desiderius Erasmus (1466–1536), perhaps the most influential humanist in northern Europe, entered the Augustinian order as a young man, but later obtained a papal dispensation that allowed him to live outside the monastery and devote himself to scholarship. He studied at Paris but conceived a strong dislike for scholastic theology and left the university without a degree. A doctorate in theology was later conferred on him *per saltum* (that is, without passing the usual examinations) by the University of Turin. He travelled and made friends in England and Italy; at the time of the Reuchlin affair he was a resident of Louvain. He was sympathetic toward the Reformation in its early stages, but withdrew his support once the schismatic nature of Luther's movement became apparent.

Erasmus was one of the great champions of language studies and a pioneer in applying philological principles to the scriptural text. His edition of the New Testament (1516), which contained the first printed Greek text to appear on the market, was hailed by humanists and attacked by conservative theologians. His subsequent entanglement with the theologians of Louvain and Paris was often compared by his contemporaries to Reuchlin's controversies with the theologians of Cologne.

The following excerpts from two letters, in which Erasmus comments on the Reuchlin Affair, are translated from the Latin text in *Opus Epistolarum Des. Erasmi Roterodami*, ed. P.S. Allen (Oxford, 1906–58). An English translation of Erasmus's correspondence can be found in *The Collected Works of Erasmus* (Toronto, 1965– ).

## 1. Epistle 334

In 1515, after Reuchlin's case had been remanded to the papal court, Erasmus wrote to Cardinal Domenico Grimani, enlisting his help for Reuchlin. Grimani (1461–1523) was a patron of learning and a powerful presence at the papal court. Erasmus reports on his own researches and forthcoming books and expresses his appreciation for the cardinal's patronage. He continues:

And I will not be discouraged from my undertaking as long as I am supported by your favour and that of men like you, for you know that there is a long history of ill will, more noxious than any viper, hissing against excellent initiatives. And it was not without deep sadness that I saw an example of this recently in the experience of that great man, Johann Reuchlin. It would certainly be appropriate, it would certainly be high time that a man of his venerable age should enjoy his most noble studies and reap a sweet harvest from the honest seed of his youthful labour. It would be only right that a man who is equipped with so many languages and knowledge in so many disciplines should in the autumn of his life disseminate the rich product of his intellect to the whole world. To this end he should have been exhorted with praise, invited with rewards, and encouraged with support. And I hear that certain men have appeared on the scene, who themselves are incapable of producing anything great but seek glory through the most perverse means. Immortal God, what a great tragedy they make of frivolous nonsense! What a fuss they have raised over a little book, a letter rather, and that written in German, which Reuchlin never published himself and never intended for publication! Who would ever have known of its existence, if these men had not published it for the world to read? If it contained errors (and all human beings err), how much more conducive to peace would it have been to suppress it or put an innocent interpretation on it, or to forgive a man of great virtues. I am not saying this because I see any errors there; indeed, it is the task of other people to pronounce on this. I shall say only: if anyone were to inspect the books of St Jerome with such ill will (or, as the Greeks say, *apotomos*, relentlessly), he would find many things that are greatly at variance with the decrees of our theologians. What good was it to make this sort of trouble for a man who should be honoured on account of his writings and his age, and to do so for reasons of no importance, and make him waste seven years (I believe) on this? I wish he had been allowed to spend his efforts and his time on research promoting honourable studies! As it is, a man who is worthy of all rewards is involved in the most harrowing lawsuits, to the grief and irritation of all learned men, indeed of all Germany. Yet we all have hope that with your assistance this excellent man can be restored to the world and to letters.

## 2. Epistle 694

The measured tone Erasmus uses in this formal letter to a patron contrasts sharply with the emotional language he uses in a letter to his friend Willibald Pirckheimer in which he reacts to the latter's defence of Reuchlin (see above, Document 7). The Latin text of the following excerpt is in P.S. Allen, *Opus Epistolarum Des. Erasmi Roterodami* (Oxford, 1906–58), Ep. 694.

I was very pleased with your booklet in which you defend Reuchlin like a friend and speak with more than usual eloquence. For I believe Fabius is right when he says[1] that it is the heart as much as intelligence and learning that make a man eloquent. But in my opinion nothing is more unfortunate than to carry on a war indiscriminately; and just as unfortunate if it happens that one must fight a mean and shameful enemy. For who are the men with whom Reuchlin must fight? A nest of hornets whom the Roman pontiff himself would fear to provoke. In such a situation Alexander[2] used to say that he regarded it safer to give offence to one of the most powerful kings than to any one of the mendicants, who under cover of a lowly name rule over the Christian world like tyrants.[3] Yet I believe that this happens on the initiative of a few vicious men, and it is unfair to blame the whole order for it.

Consider, moreover, the tool these false professors of true religion are using: a man who is a layman, who has no shame, and who can hardly be called a half-Jew, for his actions show that he is a Jew and a half whom no kind of misdeed could make worse than he already is. Could the devil, that eternal enemy of the Christian religion, have wished for a better tool than this angel of Satan transformed into an angel of light, who under the pretext of defending religion disturbs the peace and concord of the Christian commonwealth everywhere – peace which is the principal good of the Christian religion? What can be more unworthy for men who deserve to be immortalized than to fight with such a monster? His very name, I believe, would dirty the paper on which it is written. My life upon it: that fellow chose to be baptized for no other reason than to be in a better position to destroy Christianity, and by mixing with us, infect the whole people with his Jewish poison. For what harm could he have inflicted, if he had remained a Jew? But now that he has put on the mask of the Christian, he truly plays the Jew. Now at last he is true to his race. They have slandered Christ, but Christ only. He raves against many upright men of proven virtue and learning. He could not have done a more welcome favour to his fellow Jews than pretending to be an apostate and betraying the Christian cause to the enemy. He is as useless as a stone in everything else, and talented only when it comes to slander. What sacrifice could have been more pleasing to Satan than his sowing the seeds of discord among Christians everywhere?

Whence does Satan derive his name in Hebrew? From 'opposing' of course.[4] Does Pfefferkorn not resemble him, when he cries out again and opposes men who work for the public welfare, when he uses his criminal methods against them and believes that he is born for this business alone? Whence does the devil take his name in Greek? Not from usury, not from adultery, not from theft, or any other vice, but from slander.[5] Is he not an apostle of the devil, when he has dedicated his whole life to this effort: to defame and slander the names of excellent men before the unlearned people? He abuses the name of religion to commit a crime. This is not the deed of just any demon, but the trick of the most cunning devil. He knows he cannot please scholars and good men; he knows he cannot easily deceive them. For this reason he lays his complaints before the unlearned people, he blathers among superstitious women who, as Paul says, are burdened with sins, and has found fertile ground for his evil seed. He uses magnificent words to deceive them, declaiming before them about 'the defence of the Christian religion,' about 'heresies and excommunications.' The people are too stupid to notice the prowling wolf hiding under sheep's clothing.

Oh criminal 'corn,' so dissimilar from that which fell on the earth and brought forth the food of life! This corn has been sown by the devil's hand. It is the seed of hemlock or whatever is more poisonous than hemlock. If we are not alert and do not watch out, he will inject the fatal poison of dissent into Christian concord. For what will happen if this slanderer is allowed to rage in this manner against all who are unlike him? And if learned men are forced to write books in response to this filthy creature? Believe me, my learned Willibald, this is just the beginning and will go further than the common people perhaps realize. We see that sometimes a huge fire arises from a small spark.

I am surprised, moreover, that the bishops are not more vigilant in this matter, that they do not burn this monster while there is time and take action against the poison which takes effect everywhere and has infected everything. This wretched slanderer cannot be defeated, for he is entirely made up of malice and has so many demons that breathe new vigour into him, when he is exhausted. Therefore he will never be defeated with abuse, for it is his main ambition to have his name perpetuated in the books of scholars and be made famous in posterity. This is what this cursed fellow is thinking: I may be unpopular with a few good and learned men, but I am satisfied if I please the majority. If my tricks are discovered and my plots become known, I may be denounced by all Christians, but I will certainly attain glory among my fellow Jews. For they will realize then that I did not desert them out of malice. It is therefore not only shameful but indeed useless for scholars to fight him, for they can gain nothing by it except infamy – whether they win or lose the battle. It would be better for an executioner to put an end to this madness. But this is the task of bishops, the task of the most just Emperor Maximilian, the task of the authorities of the famous city of Cologne. They must not nourish this poisonous viper, who will bring certain destruction on the Christian religion; rather they must offer an antidote to this great evil. And I speak not from any personal resentment, for he has never harmed me, or at any rate, if he has blathered anything against me, it leaves me quite unmoved and unconcerned. But I am grieved to see that the unity of the Christian people has been destroyed in this unworthy fashion by the manoeuvers of one profane and boorish Jew, and that he has been helped by men who claim to be the pillars of the Christian religion.

**Notes**

1 Fabius Quintilian, *Institutiones oratoriae*, 10.4.15.
2 Presumably a reference to Pope Alexander VI (1430–1503).
3 'Mendicants,' i.e., 'beggars,' referring to the intention of their founders who wished them to remain poor and live off charitable gifts. By the sixteenth century, the profession of poverty was a sham, and the mendicants wielded great power through their inquisitorial activities.
4 As explained, for example, by the Church Father St Basil in *Homily* 9.9.
5 Erasmus uses the word *diabolus*, which is related to Greek *diabole*, slander.

## DOCUMENT 10

# The Dedicatory Letter of Reuchlin's *De arte cabalistica*, 1517

The first-fruit of Reuchlin's cabalistic studies was the dialogue *On the Wonder-working Word* (1494),[1] which attempts a synthesis of Christian and Jewish mysticism. He followed this up in 1517 with another dialogue entitled *De arte cabalistica* (On the Art of the Cabala), printed by Thomas Anshelm in Hagenau. The book, which introduces a Jew, a Pythagorean philosopher, and a Muslim as speakers, was intended as a justification of cabalistic studies. During the intervening decades, Reuchlin had become proficient in Hebrew and had read a number of cabalistic texts. The book, published at a time when Reuchlin's lawsuit in Rome was still pending, serves as a plea for the preservation of Jewish books and a legitimization of Reuchlin's interests.

Reuchlin dedicated the book to Pope Leo X (Giovanni de' Medici, 1475–1521, Pope Leo X from 1513). The son of the Medici ruler, Lorenzo the Magnificent, Giovanni de' Medici was tutored by the famous humanist Angelo Poliziano and studied Greek under Bernardo Michelozzi. He entered the church and was made a cardinal in 1489 by Innocent VIII, who was a relative by marriage. From 1489–92 he studied at the University of Pisa and obtained a doctorate in canon law. He undertook a number of diplomatic missions for the papal court and travelled widely for pleasure and education. He was an important champion of the arts and of the New Learning, patronizing Michelangelo and Raphael, making the University of Rome an intellectual centre, and increasing the holdings of the Vatican Library. Today, however, he is perhaps better known as the pope who excommunicated Luther.

The following text, the dedicatory letter and conclusion of *De arte cabalistica*, is translated from the facsimile edition published by the Friedrich

Frommann Verlag (Stuttgart, 1964). The Latin text appears on pp. 111–12 and 270–1. An English translation of the complete work was published by M. and S. Goodman, New York, 1983.

To His Holiness Leo X, Supreme Pontiff of the Christian religion: Italian philosophy derives from an ancient tradition. It was handed down to great men of outstanding intellect by its founder, Pythagoras. Over the years, however, it was ruined by carping sophists and buried in the darkness of a black night until, by God's grace, the famous Lorenzo de Medici, your father, the prince of Florence and the descendent of the great Cosimo,[2] arose and shone his light on every field of liberal studies. We know that he showed such ability in ruling the republic and wisely and prudently handling affairs at home as well as on campaigns that no one in his age deserved higher praise in politics, but when we add to this his language skills, we must admit that his birth was auspicious and heaven-sent. After Petrarch, Filelfo, and Aretino[3] – men of letters who taught the youth of Florence the discipline of eloquence and the art of speaking well, so that the citizens of Florence were undisputedly superior to other nations in calligraphy and in purity of style – it was Lorenzo who introduced to his fatherland that force which drives out vice and that method of investigating the wisdom of old, which had lain hidden until his time in the books and monuments of antiquity. For this task he gathered the greatest scholars from everywhere, the greatest experts in ancient literature, who were as eloquent as they were knowledgeable: Demetrius Chalcondyles, Marsilio Ficino, Georgio Vespucci, Christophoro Landino, Valori, Angelo Poliziano, Giovanni Pico count of Mirandola, and the rest of the world's best scholars.[4] Through them the wisdom of the ancients, which the evils of time had lost or hidden, was restored to the light of day. These excellent men vied with one another. One taught, another wrote commentaries, or read, or interpreted, or translated. Marsilio [Ficino] introduced Greek to Italy, Poliziano led the Romans back to Greece. Each one laboured over his task, everyone brought great honour to the Medici. By divine fortune, it was among them that you were born, that your shoot, so to speak, grew up, Holy Father, so that there might be no field in the humanities in which you would not become learned, for even as a boy you embraced the smooth style of the urbane Poliziano. Need I say more? No city at that time was more flourishing than Florence. There the humanities, which had perished completely, were reborn. There were no language arts, no literary studies that were not practised by the noble Florentines. Touched by her fame I was seized by a desire to see the city, not only the magnificent palace of your grandfather, Cosimo the Great – built in a magnificent style unknown to us northerners – but also to see your parent, the man who was the source of such blessings in our century.

Thus I set out for Italy with the illustrious Duke Eberhard Probus,[5] an outstanding man in our time, whose secretary I was. We entered Florence around 20 March 1482 AD. Since I had praised the noble Medicis to my duke, as I was in truth obliged to do, he expressed the wish to speak with them. When someone brought this to Lorenzo's attention he extended his hospitality to us strangers in a most humane way and led us all to his house, showing us all the remarkable sights: first, the well-built stables for the horses, then the armory well stocked with weapons, afterwards the individual rooms hung with precious tapestries and beautiful carpets, and on the open roof a forest of trees, the garden of the Hesperides[6] and the golden apples. I praised his library to the skies, and that urbane man answered in the most gentlemanly fashion that his children were a greater treasure than his books. I beg you, Holy Father, let a man of the people like myself be frank with you: Can you imagine how lost I was in admiration and how joyful when I was told, among universal applause, that you had reached the highest pinnacle of honour, you the best son of the best and wisest prince, the saintly Lorenzo Medici! I suddenly recalled the prophetic words of your father, who was like a true prophet, saying: Fruit borne of the Laurentian laurel is precious not only for Lorenzo's people but for the whole world. Could anything be a greater treasure than your ineffable reign, from which riches flow like gold from the bed of the river Pactolus:[7] the charm and graces of literature and all that is good in humanity. Your father sowed the seeds of universal ancient philosophy which are now growing to maturity under your reign so that the ears of this corn can be harvested in all languages: Greek, Latin, Hebrew, Arabic, Chaldaic, and Chaldaean. For Your Majesty offers in these days books in these languages and everything begun under your father flourishes more abundantly under your reign.

Noticing that scholars were lacking only Pythagoras,[8] who is enjoyed by only a few in the Laurentian academy, I thought it might give you pleasure if I brought into the public realm the beliefs of Pythagoras and the noble Pythagoreans, so that what has been unknown so far, may be read in Latin under your patronage. In Italy Marsilio [Ficino] published Plato, in France Lefèvre d'Etaples restored Aristotle.[9] I, Reuchlin, will join their number and exhibit to the Germans a reborn

Pythagoras, dedicated to your name. This could not have been done without the Hebrew cabala, for the Pythagorean philosophy has its origin in it, and with the memory of the roots being lost, it entered the books of the cabalists again via Greater Greece. Thus everything had to be searched out again. I have therefore written of the symbolic philosophy of the art of the cabala to make Pythagorean teaching better known to scholars. But in all this I myself make no assertions;[10] I merely recount the opinions of a third party. They are non-Christians: the Jew Simon, an experienced cabalist, who is on his way to Frankfurt, meets at an inn on the way a Pythagorean by the name of Philolaus the Younger and a Muslim by the name of Marranus. They have put away their luggage and are hungry for a meal but they dislike the motley crowd of drinkers and leave the tavern after dinner. And thus begins their conversation.

[The dialogue follows. It concludes with another appeal to Leo X and a specific reference to the ongoing court case. Reuchlin explains that the principal purpose of his work is scholarly; however, he was also looking for distraction from the weary battle he had been fighting for the past five years; and third, he wanted to offer Leo a token of his gratitude.]

Let this be in memory of your benevolence, in memory of the many times when your fatherly care broke up the intrigues of my enemies and protected me from them. For they do not cease (I know) to importune your pious ears, sometimes through hired agents, at other times through their letters, such as I understand were sent to you last September 18 from Cologne, whose title is lying even about the author's name.[11] For it is not the University of Cologne, which I respect, that is behind this; specific men, a dirty clique of enemies, a small segment and all the more insane, have done this to persuade Your Holiness of what is not true, counter to the apostolic command, counter to the peace decreed by the emperor. You see that they have the audacity to instruct you in their letters, laying down laws like Solon,[12] presuming to teach you, the source of justice, how one ought to proceed with the trial according to their beck and call. Their aim is to achieve a sordid victory over me, as if my innocence were not already obvious to the whole world. I cannot therefore bring myself to believe that you have faith in these men, who have disregarded the apostolic prohibition, have despised your censure, and without due legal process burned my book while the case was still pending. Rather, you will put your trust in important men from Upper Germany,[13] for every great man there agrees that I have caused no scandal and have given no opening for the destruction of any people in Germany, who are after all linked with me by our common language – a language unknown to those people in the Netherlands.[14] I published my counsel, which was given in confidence, together with a plain explanation in a book, as is proper, and you may put your trust in it, all the more so as you have received confirmation of my innocence in many sealed and trustworthy letters. My innocence, piety, faith, and integrity have been attested by many illustrious rulers over large territories in our nation, by magistrates, by German communities, the cities in the holy dioceses of our bishops. You have in your hands testimony, three-fold and four-fold, from the invincible Roman elector, Emperor Maximilian to Maximoleon,[15] ... [more references follow] ... All of them confirm that I caused no scandal anywhere through my writings. On the contrary, I was building and planting in the church the seedlings of diverse languages in the Holy Spirit, who has gathered all peoples speaking diverse languages into one faith. They recognize that I was the first of all men to introduce Greek to Germany, first of all to give and hand down to the universal church Hebrew language skills and studies, and I hope that I shall not hope in vain when I believe that my services to the church will be welcome to future generations and that I shall be given the peace and quiet I deserve for my long and hard service in the interest of the orthodox faith, under your reign, Most Blessed Leo, Supreme Pontiff, who judges on the basis of facts rather than words. But if you really wish to subject my life to the perpetual persecutions of evil men, I shall be very glad to be deemed worthy to suffer such injustice for our Christ.

**Notes**

1 See above, p. 15.
2 Lorenzo the Magnificent (1449–92) and his grandfather Cosimo (1389–1464) are the most famous members of the Medici family, merchant bankers and rulers of Florence in the Renaissance.
3 Petrarch (1304–74), best known for his *Canzoniere* celebrating his love for Laura, is regarded as the father of the Italian Renaissance; Francesco Filelfo (1398–1481), pioneer of Greek studies, taught in Florence from 1429 to 1435 (see above, p. 107, n. 13); the designation 'Aretino' (of Arezzo) was used of a number of Italian humanists. Reuchlin may have had in mind Francesco Griffolini Aretino (1420–after 1465) or Rinuccio Aretino. Both

men produced translations from the Greek. Alternatively, he may have meant the poet Bernardo Accolti Aretino (1458–1535).

4 Demetrius Chalcondyles (1423–1511), a Greek emigré, taught Greek in Florence from 1475. Angelo Poliziano and Giovanni Pico della Mirandola were among his students. Marsilio Ficino (1433–1499), the Neoplatonist philosopher, was patronized by Cosimo and saw Lorenzo actively involved in his so-called 'Platonic Academy.' Giorgio Vespucci (1434–1514) was a member of the Platonic Academy. Cristoforo Landino (c. 1424–98), poet, academic, politician, taught literature and rhetoric in Florence. 'Valori' could be either Baccio Valori, who belonged to Ficino's circle, or Niccolo Valori (1464–1526), best known today as a correspondent of Machiavelli.

5 Eberhard the Bearded of Würtemberg, d. 1496.

6 Mythological guardians of a tree with golden apples, used in poetical language for 'oranges.'

7 River in ancient Lydia, famed for its gold.

8 Sixth-century BC sage, whose name is associated with religious and scientific traditions. He left no writings. His religious ideas were associated with Jewish religion from the third century BC (first by Hermippus of Smyrna), but the connection is spurious.

9 For Ficino, see n. 4. Jacques Lefèvre d'Etaple (c. 1460–1536) taught at Paris. He published commentaries and editions of Aristotelian works. In later life he became involved with the reformist movement at Meaux and devoted himself to biblical studies and translations of the Bible into French. These activities brought him into conflict with the theological faculty of Paris and led to the accusation of heterodoxy.

10 He is referring to the fact that the book is not written in the first person but cast in the form of a dialogue.

11 Not identified.

12 Famous Athenian lawgiver from the sixth century BC.

13 Perhaps a reference to the *Letters of Famous Men*. See above, Document 5.

14 Perhaps a reference to the condemnation of the *Eye Mirror* by the University of Louvain or to Hoogstraten, a native of Antwerp and graduate of the University of Louvain.

15 Maximilian (meaning 'greatest soldier'); Maximoleo (meaning 'greatest Leo' or 'Lion'), a word play.

**DOCUMENT 11**

# Jacob Hoogstraten

## *Information to the Reader*, 1519

Jacob Hoogstraten (d. 1527) was a graduate of the University of Louvain (MA, 1485), where he also taught for a while. He then entered the Dominican order and studied theology at Cologne (doctorate, 1504). He was prior of the Dominican convent in Cologne, a member of the faculty of theology at Cologne, and from 1510 on inquisitor of the archdioceses of Cologne, Mainz, and Trier. He became involved in a controversy with the humanist and jurist Peter of Ravenna and was instrumental in forcing him to leave Cologne in 1508. His role in the Reuchlin controversy is outlined above, pp. 20–2. After his appeal to the papal court was prorogued, he returned to Cologne and published an *Apologia* (Cologne, 1518), consisting of three sections: a list of 'heretical' passages excerpted from Reuchlin's *Eye Mirror*; passages from Reuchlin's *Defence* and his rebuttals; and a dialogue between Hoogstraten and a defender of Reuchlin, Georgius Benignus, who had been a member of the Roman commission appointed by Pope Leo X to examine the Reuchlin affair.[1] The last section was also, in part, a reaction to Willibald Pirckheimer's defence of Reuchlin.[2] In response, Count Hermann of Neuenahr, a champion of Reuchlin, published a collection of three letters under the title *Epistolae trium illustrium virorum* (Letters of Three Famous Men, Cologne, 1518). The letters, written by Reuchlin, Buschius, and Hutten, were addressed to Neuenahr. Neuenahr added a letter of his own to Reuchlin, which served as a preface to the collection, and furthermore appended a tract entitled 'A new defence of Johann Reuchlin, brought here from Rome.' The latter circulated in Rome in 1516 under the name 'Johannes.' The author has not been identified. Hoogstraten responded to the *Letters of Three Famous Men* with an *Apologia Secunda* (Second Apologia, Cologne,

1519), which he dedicated to the papal protonotary, Johann Ingenwinkel. The dedicatory letter is followed by an 'Information to the Reader' which is translated here from the Latin text in Böcking, *Supplementum*, I:434–8. Hoogstraten's style, which is ridiculed in Buschius's letter, is convoluted and does not always yield a clear meaning.

## *Information to the Reader*

Pious Reader: It is now seven years since a number of doctors of theology at various well-known universities and Johann Reuchlin, a Swabian doctor of laws and a great orator, were requested by imperial mandate to offer their counsel. The advice sought was not 'Advice on whether the Jews should be deprived of all their books and whether they should be destroyed and burned,'[3] as Reuchlin has it in the title of his *Eye Mirror*; rather, the question was what should be decided and what should best be done about certain Jewish books that corrupted God's sacred mysteries, and blasphemed against Christ and the church. Let Reuchlin explain why he treats on the same side of the same page a question that is very different and which may or may not have come from the emperor. Wishing to appear more distinguished than the others, Reuchlin far exceeded the boundaries of a Catholic consultation (going beyond the imperial commission, for His Imperial Majesty never asked whether all Jewish books were to be burned, as can be seen from his mandate) and published on his private initiative a book containing his counsel, which he entitled *Eye Mirror*. This book came into my hands, not in my capacity as a member of the Dominican order or prior of the Cologne monastery, but in my capacity as inquisitor of heretical pravity for three provinces,[4] to which I was appointed by the apostolic see. On a formal request and in accordance with my office I examined the book and found it full of pernicious pravity, and containing numerous errors that cannot be tolerated by the church. My judgment was publicly confirmed by that of doctors from the most famous universities, etc. The case therefore was referred to Rome and soon (I omit many unimportant matters for the sake of brevity) adjourned to an opportune time. Last year there appeared a dialogue attributed to Georgius Benignus of Nazareth,[5] printed and published in defence of Reuchlin, to which I responded sufficiently last Easter in my *First Apologia*. Truth being my guide, I answered him line by line. However, when Reuchlin, a very sharp-tongued man, and his followers realized that, contrary to their expectations, they were not able to counter our rational argumentation and Catholic decisions with their attacks, they proceeded to insults and invectives full of iniquity and lies, etc. Apart from that, I have received no answer from them except a quite ridiculous pamphlet that you can see below by a 'Johannes' who has no last name,[6] written in Rome two years ago and recently published in our city of Cologne as if it were a new defensive weapon of Reuchlin's ... What then can be more shameful and indecent, what could be more ridiculous for Johann Reuchlin than to publish old material, and to publish it without making clear who the author is? ... I will not dwell on the fact that the imprint was flawed and will say nothing about the finale of that book. I am offended not only by the latter, but by the fact that the charges which I have brought against Reuchlin in Rome in a legal and proper form have been ineptly passed over in this book. To the present day the author evades these legitimate, true charges. He takes up the bow and arrow, but does not point it at the target, at which he should aim. When I realized this, I thought of the verse in Horace: 'The mountains heave, and a ridiculous mouse is born.'[7] But let us proceed, keeping away from contumely and insults, in the manner of wise men.

Some three years ago I received some objections from the hand of the reverend lord cardinal of St Eusebius[8] against the counsel (written in German) or *Eye Mirror* of Johann Reuchlin, which the reverend later told me he had given to the solicitors of Reuchlin. After a long delay, after repeatedly addressing the cardinal and pointing out that, since he had given to the adversaries documents that concerned me, he should oblige them to respond, after much begging, and with great difficulty I finally achieved that much. When their reponse ... was handed to me by the reverend in the city [of Rome], I shortly replied and responded, and presented my replications (as I will call them) to the judge with my respects, but this response was omitted in their booklet. The author of the response, that is, Reuchlin's defender, that obscure man who wants to obscure his name and person, is therefore quite defective. He cites my objections defectively, introduces intolerable errors everywhere, deliberately omits material, and this is how it appeared in Cologne. It is for this reason, for the honour of Jesus Christ and our holy faith, and for no other reason, that I have published this book, which I rightly call *Second Apologia*, so that one might clearly see from it what is at issue in this battle between the church of God and Reuchlin and his unnamed defender, and that every good man may realize that I am acting not from malice but on behalf of the faith. At the beginning [of my apologia] I therefore quote Reuchlin's assertion in favour of the

Jews, word for word and in the form in which it was exhibited and accurately cited by his adversaries in Rome. Second, I add the replies of his opponents on my behalf against the objections of Reuchlin. Third, I cite the defenceless and frivolous defensive argument of that would-be defender Johannes without a surname, which I should call shenanigans rather than frivolities and which contain nothing erudite or true. Not surprisingly, for the same tripartition was earlier on observed in Rome, which these garrulous authors have given no attention whatsoever, reprinting them in incomplete form, [including] merely a few sections from one part and studiously omitting the rest, so that they might give the appearance to readers who are not aware of this manoeuvre that they have given some answer on behalf of Reuchlin. By the grace of God I have noticed this grievous deception (i.e., the omission of the third section, as indicated above) and reprint it here in my apologia. Fourth, and finally, I add the just and well-deserved reproaches of the theologians and their catholic and in every respect true allegations against that obscure Reuchlinist and would-be defender, hoping to destroy and suppress the manifold tricks of that unnamed defender. Do not be angry with me, modest and well-meaning reader (or any other upright man) because I call the would-be defender sometimes garrulous, at other times a sophist, a cheater, a back-handed fellow or by other names. For the following will show that all the epithets I used are fair, and even stronger terms are called for, especially when we see that no proper author's name appears with this puerile publication ...

As for the rest, learned reader, I believe that some people may criticize my work and say perhaps, in their characteristic slanderous tone, that the style of this work is not Latin, that it is written by an illiterate man, as someone recently dared to assert in a published letter to a noble count.[9] What shall I say to that? Such is the wanton fantasy or rather blindness of some people, who feel nauseated by the nourishment of Christ, that they do not deign to take notice of the most fertile truth, unless it is spoken in splendid Ciceronian style. The apostle's word will sufficiently answer them, if I may cite it in my defence: 'I may be rude in speech but not in knowledge.' And elsewhere: 'I have not come with subtle words.' And again: 'I do not speak in the enticing words of human wisdom, but in the teaching of the Spirit.'[10] For I strive for the truth, which the Holy Spirit expressed, and am intent on holy scripture, not verbal pomp. And splendid style has no place in this work and cannot be expected from a text that cites speakers verbatim. It is my principal aim to escape the slander of captious and malicious men, to cite Reuchlin's words faithfully and only in the translation that was submitted on behalf of the opponents during the judicial process in Rome, a translation by Martin Groningen,[11] who is otherwise a literate man but did not aim at rhetorical flourishes here and used a simple style. And I shall do likewise in answering the words of the defender, whose style is much inferior to the other man's. For this reason I am not aiming for ornate style in this work, for I know very well that it is written: one must not hitch an ox and a donkey together at the plough, and one must not wear clothing that is made of a mixture of wool and linen[12] ... I presume to answer their insults in accordance with my office and in a theological style, for I do not wish to involve the business of faith in malicious contention (as I wrote in the preceding letter addressed to the reverend, the lord bishop of Xanten,[13] who cannot be praised highly enough). For it is characteristic of heretics and of those who undertake to defend heretical books or heretics themselves, that they are powerless when it comes to argumentation and citation of ecclesiastical verdicts and therefore defend themselves somehow or other with abuse, execrations, and quibbling arguments, and even action (if they can). Farewell, pious reader, and take the following work in good part, for it is written succinctly in a straightforward manner, in honour of our Lord Jesus Christ, and for the salvation of all faithful. Cologne, at our convent, August 1518.

**Notes**

1 See above, p. 21.
2 See Document 8.
3 The title is quoted in German; Hoogstraten's Latin translation adds, however, 'without any exceptions.'
4 See above, headnote.
5 The titular archbishop of Nazareth, Juraj Dragisic (1445–1520), known by his latinized name as Georgius Benignus. He was a member of the papal commission examining Reuchlin's *Eye Mirror* and wrote an apologia on his behalf, entitled *Defensio praestantissimi viri Joannis Reuchlin* (Cologne, 1517).
6 See above, headnote.
7 Horace, *Ars poetica*, 136
8 In Rome the Reuchlin case proceeded under the direction of Cardinals Domenico Grimani and Pietro Accolti.
9 Hutten to Neuenahr, text in Böcking, *Supplementum*, I, 164–8.
10 I Cor. 1:17, 2:4; II Cor. 11:6.

11 Martin Groningen (or Gröning, d. 1521), was a jurist (doctorate in law from the University of Siena). He was in Rome in 1515 and translated the *Eye Mirror* into Latin on Reuchlin's behalf. He reported on the progress of the law suit to Reuchlin.

12 Metaphorically, an injunction against unsuitable combinations. Cf. Deut. 22: 11–12.

13 Johann Ingenwinkel (1469–1535), an influential man at the Roman curia.

## DOCUMENT 12

# Hutten's Letters to Erasmus and Reuchlin, 1520/1

When Luther became the leading voice among those who demanded church reform, many humanists supported his cause. Ulrich von Hutten[1] was one of his most fervent champions, although his aims were political as well as religious. Erasmus, by contrast, was cautious in his support. He feared a schism and wanted to keep humanistic studies out of the dispute.[2] In spite of his efforts, humanism became associated with the Reformation in the eyes of many observers. Indeed, Catholic theologians tended to see humanists, and Erasmus in particular, as the inspirational sources of the Reformation.

Hutten, who realized that it was in the interest of the reformers to maintain a common front with humanists, wrote to Erasmus in 1520, pleading with him to speak up on Luther's behalf or at any rate to keep any misgivings to himself. He hinted that the humanities, too, would benefit from this policy. A few months later, in February 1521, Hutten wrote a similar letter to Reuchlin, reproaching him for criticizing the reformers openly. The excerpts from his letters to Erasmus are translations from the Latin text in Allen, Epp. 1135 and 1161. Both letters remained unpublished during Erasmus's lifetime; Erasmus's response is not extant. The Latin text of Hutten's letter to Reuchlin is in Böcking, *Supplementum*, II: 803–4.

### 1. Epistle 1135 to Erasmus

I ask you to keep quiet and restrain your pen, for we need you safe. Listen to what I say to you, trusting in our friendship. While the

Reuchlin affair was disputed with great heat, you seemed to be fearful and showed more weakness than was worthy of you[3] ... So I am asking you now, as one of your long-standing supporters who still wants your good opinion, if at all possible: do not write anything unguardedly as we have seen you do in the cases of Luther and Reuchlin. You know how triumphant our enemies were. And they are still carrying around with them certain letters of yours, in which you avoid unpopularity yourself and devolve it on others in a hateful manner. This was the way in which you killed off the *Letters of Obscure Men*, a book that you used to like a great deal. And in Luther you condemn the fact that he has touched the untouchable, while you yourself have done the same everywhere in earlier writings. Yet you will not be successful in making them believe that you do not very much want [this reform] to happen. In this way you hurt us and do not please them. In fact you irritate them and arouse their hostility by dissimulating what is obvious. As for my own affairs, there could be nothing more splendid than having you write in my support, but if you do not want to load yourself down with unpopularity, make at least one concession to me: do not allow fear to force you into making light of it. Better pass it over in complete silence. For I know what great harm a word of yours could do me, if in your writings you appear either to argue against my plan or at any rate to disapprove of it.

I have written this frankly, as to a friend. Farewell, from the stronghold of the Huttens, 15 August 1520.

**2. Epistle 1161, November 1520, to Erasmus**

[Luther's opponents claim] that you are the author of all of this, that you are the fountain from which everything flows that now troubles Leo.[4] You were the forerunner, you taught us, they say, you first kindled in men's minds a zeal for liberty, you are the man on whom the rest of us depends. Even if that is not the case, you know the kind of people with whom we are dealing here and you must not harbour hopes that you are safe where you are. In this affair, liberal studies have attracted hatred, and the man who introduced them and filled Germany with learning incurs even worse hatred. Tell me, what do you make of the letter the cardinal of Tortosa wrote to Number Ten,[5] expostulating with him for tolerating you in Germany – you, who taught us these things? ... If you cannot approve my plan, you cannot disapprove the reason behind my attempt to free Germany. For once Germany is free, liberal studies, too, will flourish and be held in honour. A difficult thing to achieve, you say. Yes, very difficult, but attempting it is honourable, whatever the outcome ... I am convinced that this is the time destined for me to incur danger for my country's sake ... My advice to you is not to make so much of your precious ease and not to persuade yourself that you will be left in peace in this most dangerous situation.

### 3. Hutten's letter to Reuchlin

Ulrich Hutten to his friend Johann Reuchlin, greetings: I have read your letter ... in which you respond to the accusations of Leo X. Immortal gods, what is this! You have come to such depth of emotional weakness that you do not even abstain from speaking ill of those who have always wanted you safe and defended your reputation sometimes at great risk to themselves. Franz [von Sickingen],[6] for whom I translated your letter, could not be more upset about it. What can you possibly hope to achieve from people who have never treated you well or fairly, by destroying Luther's cause, if that were in your power? Have you not learned in nine years what can be got from them with flattery? Even if your stated disapproval of Luther could rescue you from them, you cannot regard it as honest to oppose his party, when you see that men belong to it whom you must always support in a respectable cause, unless you want to be the most ungrateful man of all. It would have been sufficient if you had written in your defence that you had never had anything to do with Luther, as Erasmus wrote. No, you had to add that you have always disapproved of his cause, that you have taken it very ill that your name should be found in his writings, that you tried to warn us off – us who are Luther's followers. With such shameful flattery you hope to soften them, to whom you should not even have sent friendly greetings, if you had wanted to act like a man, for they have injured you gravely in so many unspeakable ways. Alright, soften them up. And if your age is up to it, do what you want to do most: go to Rome and kiss Lord Leo's feet. Even add (and you couldn't possibly omit it) that you will write against us. But you will see, even against your will, even if you and the pope's courtiers oppose us together: we shall cast off the shameful yoke and free ourselves from this mean servitude (for you boast that you have always gladly served, as if this were worthy of you). You do not like Luther's cause, you disapprove of it, you want to see it destroyed. Have you forgotten Franz, who has fought so bravely on your behalf? Have you forgotten me, who has stood by you to the end, even when that conflagration was at its height and blazing dangerously? Have you forgotten the others who have energetically defended you in word and deed, both because they felt sorry for you personally and also because they saw that the cause of the humanities, which we all support, is linked with yours? And you want to fight that same party, which you cannot do in good conscience and which is admittedly a crime, in the hope of achieving something that, even if it were offered, you should have qualms accepting, but (if I know them) you will not achieve even with constant flattery. Have you no confidence in Franz? Do you no longer trust in the protection of all good men? And because you lack spirit and energy, you thought we too lacked what is needed to save you. I am ashamed now of all the things I have written and done on your behalf, seeing the ugly conclusion of this affair of yours, in which we have laboured so bravely. I wanted you to know this. You can decide yourself what is fitting for you and which is better: to be grateful to your benefactors or, by acting meanly, to oblige those who always wanted your destruction. You will always find me in total disagreement with you, not so much when you fight against Luther's cause as when you submit to the Roman pontiff. Farewell, from the Ebernburg, 22 February.

**Notes**

1 See above, pp. 109–10.
2 See above, p. 141.
3 Although Erasmus did write on Reuchlin's behalf (see above, Document 9), he preferred to remain in the background. He complained about the inclusion of his letters in support of Reuchlin in the collection *Clarorum virorum epistolae* (Letters of Illustrious Men) of 1519. The earlier collection, *Letters of Famous Men*, published in 1514, contained no letter of his. It appears that Reuchlin initiated a correspondence with him only in the spring of 1514.
4 Pope Leo X.
5 'Cardinal of Tortosa' is a reference to the future Pope Adrian VI, tutor of Charles V, who was chancellor of the University of Louvain, bishop of Tortosa from 1516, cardinal from 1517, and elected to the papacy in 1522. 'Number Ten' is Pope Leo X.
6 See above, p. 24.

## DOCUMENT 13

# Two Comments by Luther on the Historical Context of the Reuchlin Affair

Martin Luther (1483–1546), whose Ninety-five Theses have become synonymous with the beginning of the Reformation, repeatedly likened his position to that of Reuchlin and Erasmus, and for a time regarded it as politic to maintain a common front with the humanists in fending off the attacks of university theologians. The following extracts show Luther constructing an historical setting for his own case. Luther took an early interest in Reuchlin's case and sided with the humanist. In 1514 he wrote to Georg Spalatin, chancellor of Elector Frederick of Saxony: 'I hold Reuchlin in great esteem ... in my opinion there is nothing in his counsel that is dangerous' (*WA* Briefe I, Ep. 7). Drawing parallels between the treatment he had received at the hands of theologians and the experiences of earlier humanists, he suggested that they were attacked for similar reasons or that they defended positions similar to his own. The first excerpt comes from Luther's *Resolutiones disputationum de indulgentiarum virtute* (Resolutions of the Dispute Regarding the Efficacy of Indulgences, 1518), in which he defends his Ninety-five Theses in a traditional scholastic manner, that is, citing numerous prooftexts from the Bible, the Fathers, and Canon Law. The work was aimed primarily at theologians, but Luther also had his eye on humanistic readers and tried to enlist their support. The second excerpt comes from the *Responsio ad condemnationem doctrinalem per Lovanienses et Colonienses factam* (Response to the Condemnation of Doctrine Issued by the Theologians of Louvain and Cologne, 1520). While the *Resolutions* are written, for the most part, in a measured tone, the *Response* uses much harsher and indeed abusive language. It is a biting attack on the theologians who had officially condemned a number of passages from Luther's writings in February 1520, branding them scandalous and heretical. The *Response*, like the *Resolutions*, is meant not only for the eyes of theologians, but also calculated to win applause from humanists.

The Latin texts of the excerpts are in *WA* I: 574 and VI: 184–5.

### 1. *Resolutions*

I hardly consider it necessary to state once again what I deny and what I assert. Since, however, the inquisitors into heretical pravity are so zealous in our time that they try to make heretics out of the most Christian Catholics, it will be pertinent to say something about each single item. Note what happened to Giovanni Pico della Mirandola, Lorenzo Valla, Peter of Ravenna, Johannes Vesalius, and most recently Johann Reuchlin and Jacques Lefèvre:[1] contrary to their intentions, their well-meant words were perverted and made out to be evil. And why did this happen? For no other reason, in my opinion, than that they neglected to explain every single syllable, so to speak. For such is the grip of simpletons and weak minds on the church today.

### 2. *Response*

Who would not find the condemnations of the Louvain and Cologne theologians ridiculous, considering that they have erred so many times in the past? Faithful God, how our excellent professors were blustering when they condemned the conclusions of Giovanni Pico, count of Mirandola, just so that they could insist that their errors were correct! And is there anyone today who does not admire his conclusions, except perhaps some old sophists in some forgotten corner who grind their teeth in silent fury? They cling to their beliefs even after they have seen the truth, and yet no judge of doctrine censures them as heretical, bold, and false. Nor are they afraid, in a similar instance, to clash with the same truth. Lorenzo Valla gave us a last glimmer of the original church or sparked a revival of it (in my opinion at least), but who among the theologians did not want to see his light put out? They accused him of being ignorant, when they were unworthy to hold his chamber pot. Indeed, books like *Chrysopassus*[2] and their brittle or rather glacial nonsense are truly nauseating when compared with Valla's works. Yet Lorenzo's fame increases every day and he is regarded today as a man whose equal we have not had in many centuries either in Italy or in the universal church, for he is a master not only in every discipline (something no *magister noster*[3] has achieved so far), but also in constant and genuine fervour for the Christian faith. What effect, then, did the authentic condemnation of the doctrinal condemnators and authenticators have other than bringing ridicule on them and greater glory for him? Then came Johann Reuchlin. His case revealed what the theologians of five universities[4] (for God's sake!) know, opine, and have in mind. It is well known that the ignominious defeat[5] they suffered at the hands of Reuchlin was galling to the theologians of Louvain and Cologne, that they are trying to save face and regain their old glory by starting the Luther affair. In his case they were not only authentic judges of doctrine in theory but also in practice, burning his books ... I shall not even mention the cases of Vesalius,[6] Lefèvre d'Etaples, and Erasmus, that ram whose horns got stuck in a wasps' nest, and many others in addition to them. For is there any outstanding intellect or any erudite scholar who does not immediately become the target of their backhanded tricks?

**Notes**

1 See above, Document 10, nn. 4 and 9 (Pico de la Mirandola, Lefèvre); Document 4, n. 16 (Peter of Ravenna); Lorenzo Valla (1401–57), renowned humanist who showed that the Donation of Constantine was a forgery and encountered further criticism for his collation of New Testament manuscripts. Vesalius is Johann Ruchrath von Wesel (d. c. 1479), a member of the cathedral chapter of Mainz, who was brought before the inquisitorial court on charges of heresy in 1479.
2 Johann Eck had published a book of this title in 1514.
3 The title of university teachers, the equivalent of 'professor.'
4 Reuchlin's *Eye Mirror* had been condemned by the universities of Louvain, Paris, Cologne, Erfurt, and Mainz.
5 The verdict of the bishop of Speyer, which acquitted Reuchlin. See above, p. 20.
6 See n. 1.

# BIBLIOGRAPHY

## Original Sources

Bucer, Martin. *Correspondance de Martin Bucer*, ed. C. Krieger and J. Rott. Vol. 1. Leiden, 1995.

*Epistolae obscurorum virorum*. Cologne, 1515; enlarged editions 1516, 1517; modern edition in H. Holborn ed., G. Stokes trans., *On the Eve of the Reformation*. New York, 1964.

Erasmus, Desiderius. *The Collected Works of Erasmus*. Toronto, 1965–.

Gratius, Ortwin. *Lamentationes obscurorum virorum*. Cologne, 1518.

– *Historica et vera enarratio iuridici processus habiti in Maguntia* in *Prenotamenta*. Cologne, 1514.

Hoogstraten, Jacob. *Apologia ... contra dialogum Georgio Benigno ... ascriptum*. Cologne, 1518.

– *Apologia Secunda ... contra defensionem quandam in favorem Ioannis Reuchlin novissime in lucem editam*. Cologne, 1519,

– *Destructio Cabalae*. Cologne, 1519.

– *Libellus accusatorius ... contra Oculare Speculum Ioannis Reuchlin*. Hagenau, 1518.

Hutten, Ulrich von. *Ulrichi Hutteni Equitis Operum Supplementum*, ed. E. Böcking. Leipzig, 1864.

Karben, Viktor von, *De vita et moribus Iudeorum*. Paris, 1511.

Luther, Martin. *Resolutiones disputationum de indulgentiarum virtute*. 1518. In *WA* 1: 530–628.

– *Responsio Lutheriana ad condemnationem doctrinalem per Magistros Nostros Lovanienses et Colonienses factam*. 1520. In *WA* 6: 181–95.

– *Dass Jesus Christus ein geborner Jude sei*. 1523. In *WA* 11: 314–36.

– *Wider die Sabbather an einen guten Freund*. 1538. In *WA* 50: 308–37.
– *Von den Juden und ihren Lügen*. (1543). In *WA* 53: 417–552.
Margarita, Antonius. *Der gantz Jüdisch glaub*. Leipzig, 1531.
Melanchthon, Philip. *Melanchthons Briefwechsel*, ed. H. Scheible. Vol. 1. Stuttgart, 1977.
Mutianus, Rufus. *Mutianus Rufus: Briefwechsel*, ed. C. Krause, in *Zeitschrift des Vereins für hessische Geschichte und Landeskunde*. Supplement IX. 1885.
Neuenahr, Hermann von. ed. *Epistolae trium virorum*. Cologne, 1518.
Nigri, Petrus. *Der Stern Meschiah*. Esslingen, 1477.
*Nizzahon: The Jewish-Christian Debate in the High Middle Ages: A Critical Edition of the Nizzahon Vetus*, ed. and trans. D. Berger. Northvale, 1996.
Pfefferkorn, Johann. *Speculum adhortationis iudaice ad Christum*. Cologne, 1507; modern edition in Kirn, 205–30.
– *Ich heyss ain buechlein der iuden peicht*. Augsburg, 1508.
– *Ich bin ain Buchlinn der Juden veindt ist mein namen*. Augsburg, 1509.
– *Wie die blinden Juden yr Ostern halten*. Cologne, 1509.
– *Handt Spiegel*. Mainz, 1511.
– *Sturm Glock*. Cologne, 1514.
– *Beschyrmung* n.p., 1516.
Pirckheimer, Willibald. *Willibald Pirckheimers Briefwechsel*, ed. D. Wuttke and H. Scheible. Munich, 1989.
Reuchlin, Johann. *Warumb die Juden so lang im ellend sind*. Pforzheim, 1505; modern edition in *Johann Reuchlin: Sämtliche Werke*, ed. W.W. Ehlers et al. Stuttgart-Bad Cannstatt, 1999, IV–1, 1–12.
– *Augenspiegel*. Tübingen, 1511; modern edition in *Johann Reuchlin: Sämtliche Werke*, ed. W.W. Ehlers et al. Stuttgart-Bad Cannstatt, 1999, IV–1, 13–64.
– *Defensio contra calumniatores suos Colonienses*. Tübingen 1513; modern edition in *Johann Reuchlin: Sämtliche Werke*, ed. W.W. Ehlers et al. Stuttgart-Bad Cannstatt, 1999, IV–1, 197–443.
– *De verbo mirifico*. 1494; modern edition in *Johann Reuchlin: Sämtliche Werke*, ed. W.W. Ehlers et al. Stuttgart-Bad Cannstatt, 1999, I–1.
– *De arte cabalistica*. Hagenau, 1517; English translation, *On the Art of the Kabbalah*, by M. and S. Goodman. New York, 1983.
– *De rudimentis Hebraicis*. Pforzheim, 1506.
– ed. *Clarorum virorum epistolae*. Tübingen, 1514.
– ed. *Illustrium virorum epistolae*. Hagenau, 1519.
– *In septem psalmos poenitentiales hebraicos interpretatio*. Tübingen, 1512.
– *Johannes Reuchlin: Gutachten über das Jüdische Schrifttum*, ed. and trans. A. Leinz-v. Dessauer. Stuttgart, 1965.
– *Recommendation Whether to Confiscate, Destroy and Burn All Jewish Books: A Classic Treatise Against Anti-Semitism*, trans. P. Wortsman. New York, 2000.

Scheurl, Christoph. *Scheurls Briefbuch*, ed. F. von Soden and J. Schnaake. Potsdam, 1867–72.

Spina, Alfonso de. *Fortalitium fidei*. Strasbourg, 1471.

*Toldot Yeshu: Das Leben Jesu nach jüdischen Quellen*, ed. S. Krauss. Hildesheim, 1977.

Vadian, Joachim. *Die Vadianische Briefsammlung der Stadtbibliothek St. Gallen*, ed. E. Arbenz and H. Wartmann. St Gallen, 1894.

**Secondary Sources**

Allen, P.S. *Opus epistolarum Des. Erasmi Roterodami*. Oxford, 1906–58.

Andernacht, D. *Regesten zur Geschichte der Juden in der Reichsstadt Frankfurt am Main von 1401-1519*. Vol. 3. Hannover, 1996.

Beitchman, P. *Alchemy of the Word: Cabala of the Renaissance*. Albany, 1998.

Benzing, J. *Bibliographie der Schriften Johannes Reuchlins im 15. und 16. Jahrhundert*. Vienna, 1955.

Blau, J. Leon. *The Christian Interpretation of the Cabala in the Renaissance*. Port Washington, WA. 1965.

Brecht, M. *Martin Luther: The Preservation of the Church*, trans. J. Schaaf. Philadelphia, 1985.

Brod, M. *Johann Reuchlin und sein Kampf: Eine historische Monographie*. Stuttgart, 1965.

Burke, P., ed. *New Perspectives on Historical Writing*. University Park, PA, 1991.

Cohen, R. *Jewish Icons: Art and Society in Modern Europe*. Berkeley, CA, 1998.

Dan, J., ed. *The Christian Kabbalah: Jewish Mystical Books and Their Christian Interpreters: A Symposium*. Cambridge, MA, 1997.

Decker-Hauff, H. 'Bausteine zur Reuchlin-Biographie.' In *Johann Reuchlin 1455–1522*, ed. M. Krebs. Pforzheim, 1955, 83–107.

Edwards, M.U. *Luther's Last Battles: Politics and Polemics, 1531–46*. Ithaca, 1983.

Erdmann-Pandzic, E., and B. Pandzic. *Eine Untersuchung zum Kampf für die jüdischen Bücher mit einem Nachdruck der 'Defensio praestantissimi viri Joannis Reuchlin' (1517) von Georgius Benignus*. Bamberg, 1989.

Foa, A. *The Jews of Europe after the Black Death*. Berkeley, CA, 2000.

Friedlaender, G., ed. *Beiträge zur Reformationsgeschichte: Sammlung ungedruckter Briefe des Reuchlin, Beza und Bullinger*. Berlin, 1837.

Geiger, J. *Johann Reuchlin: Sein Leben und seine Werke*. Leipzig, 1871; repr. Nieuwkoop, 1964.

Ginzburg, C. *The Cheese and the Worms*. Baltimore, 1980.

Graetz, H. *History of the Jews*. Vol. 4. Philadelphia, PA, 1894.

Greenblatt, S. *Renaissance Self-fashioning: From More to Shakespeare*. Chicago, 1980.

Helmrath, J. 'Humanismus und Scholastik und die deutschen Universitäten um 1500. Bemerkungen zu einigen Forschungsproblemen.' *Zeitschrift für Historische Forschung* 15 (1988): 187–203.

Herminjard, A.-L. *Correspondance des Réformateurs dans les pays de langue française*. Geneva, 1866–97.

Herzig, A., and J. Schoeps, eds. *Reuchlin und die Juden*. Sigmaringen, 1993.

Horawitz, A., and K. Hartfelder, eds. *Der Briefwechsel des Beatus Rhenanus*. Leipzig, 1886.

Joachimsen, P. 'Der Humanismus und die Entwicklung des deutschen Geistes.' *Deutsche Virteljahrsschrift für Litteraturwissenschaft und Geistesgeschichte* 8 (1980): 460–1.

Kirn, H.-M. *Das Bild vom Juden im Deutschland des frühen 16. Jahrhunderts*. Tübingen, 1989.

Kisch, G. *The Jews in Medieval Germany: A Study of Their Legal and Social Status*. Chicago, 1949.

– *Zasius und Reuchlin: Eine rechtsgeschichtlich-vergleichende Studie zum Toleranzproblem im 16. Jahrhundert*. Constance, 1961.

Kracauer, I. 'Actenstücke zur Geschichte der Confiscation der hebräischen Schriften in Frankfurt a. M.' *Monatsschrift für Geschichte der Wissenschaft des Judentums* 44 (1900): 114–26.

Krause, C. *Helius Eobanus Hessus: sein Leben und seine Werke*. Gotha, 1879.

Langmuir, G. *Toward a Definition of Antisemitism*. Berkeley, 1990.

Markish, S. *Erasmus and the Jews*, trans. A. Olcott. Chicago, 1986.

Maurer, W. 'Reuchlin und das Judentum.' In *Kirche und Geschichte: Gesammelte Aufsätze*, ed. E.-W. Kohls and G. Müller. Göttingen, 1970.

Muir, E., and G. Ruggiero, eds. *Microhistory and the Lost Peoples of Europe*. Baltimore, 1991.

Oberman, H. *The Roots of Anti-Semitism in the Age of Renaissance and Reformation*. Philadelphia, 1984.

Overdick, R. *Die rechtliche und wirtschaftliche Stellung der Juden in Südwestdeutschland im 15. und 16. Jahrhundert*. Constance, 1965.

Overfield, J. *Humanism and Scholasticism in Late Medieval Germany*. Princeton, 1984.

Peterse, H. *Jacobus Hoogstraeten gegen Johannes Reuchlin: Ein Beitrag zur Geschichte des Antijudaismus im 16. Jahrhundert*. Mainz, 1995.

Po-chia Hsia, R. *Trent 1475: Stories of a Ritual Murder Trial*. New Haven, 1992.

Po-chia Hsia, R., and H. Lehmann, eds. *In and Out of the Ghetto: Gentile-Jewish Relations in Late Medieval and Early Modern Germany*. New York, 1995.

Rummel, E. *The Humanist-Scholastic Debate in the Renaissance and Reformation.* Cambridge, MA, 1995.

Secret, F. *Les Kabbalistes chrétiens de la Renaissance.* Neuilly, 1985.

Stow, K. *Alienated Minority: The Jews of Medieval Latin Europe.* Cambridge, MA, 1992.

Weissenborn, H. *Acten der Erfurter Universität.* Halle, 1884.

Wenninger, M. *Man bedarf keiner Juden mehr: Ursachen und Hintergründe ihrer Vertreibung aus den deutschen Reichsstädten im 15. Jahrhundert.* Vienna, 1981.

White, Hayden. *Metahistory: The Historical Imagination in Nineteenth-Century Europe.* London, 1973.

Wirszubski, C. *Pico della Mirandola's Encounter with Jewish Mysticism.* Cambridge, MA, 1989.

Zika, C. *Reuchlin und die okkulte Tradition der Renaissance.* Sigmaringen, 1998.

# INDEX